the
STRANGE
CASE OF
EDWARD
GOREY

Alexander Theroux

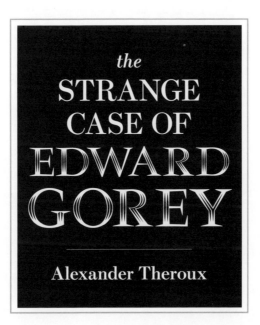

the
STRANGE
CASE OF
EDWARD
GOREY

Alexander Theroux

FANTAGRAPHICS BOOKS

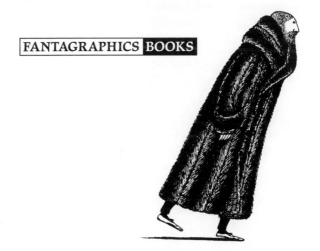

Fantagraphics Books, Inc.
7563 Lake City Way NE
Seattle, WA 98115

Edited by Gary Groth
Designed by Jacob Covey
Associate Publisher Eric Reynolds
Published by Gary Groth and Kim Thompson

Distributed in the U.S. by W.W. Norton and Company, Inc. (800-233-4830)
Distributed in Canada by Canadian Manda Group (800-452-6642 x862)
Distributed in the U.K. by Turnaround Distribution (44 020 8829-3002)
Distributed to comic book specialty stores by Diamond Comics Distributors (800-452-6642 x215)

First Fantagraphics softcover edition, August 2000
First Fantagraphics hardcover edition, January 2011
Second Fantagraphics hardcover edition, May 2011

ISBN 978-1-60699-384-2
Printed in Hong Kong

For Sarah

with love

It is a falsehood that Edward Gorey refused to give interviews. Nevertheless, to those acquainted with his hundred or so menacing little books, written as if by moonlight, the very thought of tracing out this eccentric artist (for Gorey was a solitary) might somehow have seemed to recapitulate to a nervous heart the monstrous dread felt in approaching the unholy chambers of the demented Ambrosio or the trap-doored world of the satanic Caliph Vathek of the Abassides. There is, I am saying, a specific *maledictus* about Gorey's work – little pen-and-ink cartoon marplots of delicate fright, designed, illustrated, and narrated by his own hand. Curtains are ominously pulled against intrusion. Legs protrude from ghoulish hedges. Topiary threatens. Wallpaper intimidates. It is a doomscape of scary urns, doubtful guests, black dolls, abandoned gasworks, haunted gardens, empty rooms. A silence hangs over all, admonitory and poisoned and portentous.

Gorey's is an unclassifiable genre: not really children's books, neither comic books, nor art stills. His work – sort of small and humorously sadistic parodies of the obsolete Victorian "triple decker" – comes in the form less of booklets than midget novels, each the size of a small hornbook, withered into a kind of Giacomettian reduction of twenty to thirty doomful pages of scrupulously articulated and curiously antiquarian Gothic illustration and a spare but sequential just-about-conclusive narrative, often merely wistful and understated captions of spare but distracting economy.

EG, ca. 1956, possibly at cousin Elizabeth G. Morton's graduation.

With their hand-lettering, queer layouts, their framed and ornate borders, the small books seem frightfully old-fashioned and biscuity, as if they had been secretly pressed out and printed in suspiciously limited editions in the dark, damp cellar of some creepy railway warehouse in nineteenth-century England by some old pinch-fisted joy-killer in a black claw-hammer coat with red-hot eyes, a black scowl, and a grudge against the world – and then managing to survive the must of long years by their sheer grotesquerie and horror.

Consider the Gothic novel, its evil-smelling and deliciously booby-trapped world of falling objects, unchaste noises, slipped philters, rusty locks, clanging portcullises, salivating monks, and Brueghel-like loonies with things on their minds creeping around the late-night shrubbery. Of such a world, but with so much more immaculate precision and irony, did Gorey partake, even to winnowing, by paraphrase and shrinkage, its purple prose. And the genius of his pictorial accompaniments, an odd combination of satire and irreverence that leads one to flip on almost hypnotically, supports the texts in every detail. Each page is as it were a mysterious little panel. The odd trappings Gorey employed extend even to the pseudonyms and anagrams and literary variations, outrageous and hilarious, of his own wonderfully evocative name which he so delighted in playing about with: Mrs. Regera Dowdy; D. Awdrey-Gore; Ogdred Weary; Dreary Wodge; Roy Grewdead; Edward Blutig and O Müde – two German equivalents for "Edward Gorey" and "Ogdred Weary"; Dogear Wryde; Grey Redwoad; Drew Dogyear; E. G. Deadworry; Raddory Gewe; Aedwyrd Gore; Garrod Weedy; Addée Gorrwy, Deary Rewdgo, Wee Graddory, Om, Ydora Wredge, Dedge Yarrow, Roger Addyew, Orde Graydew, Gary Dredwoe, Edgar E. Wordy, Dora Greydew, Dewda Yorger, Aedwyrd Goré, Agowy Erderd, Waredo Dyrge, Madame Groeda Weyrd – even Edward Pig!

"I wanted to publish everything under a pseudonym from the very beginning," Gorey told interviewer Robert Dahlin, "but everybody said, 'What for?' And I couldn't really explain why I wanted to. I still don't know exactly, except that I think what you publish and what you are are two different things. I really don't see that much connection."

It is the world of the shilling shocker and the penny dreadful, which Gorey so peopled and as masterfully named. Take, for example, *The Fatal Lozenge: An Alphabet* (1961), a compilation of twenty-six four-line rhymes with accompanying drawings that involves the unspeakable acts committed by cads, fetishists, lazars, proctors, hermits, undines, yeggs, zouaves, and

The Journalist *surveys the slaughter,*
The best in years without a doubt;
He pours himself a gin-and-water
And wonders how it came about.

From *The Fatal Lozenge: An Alphabet.*

Hortense was torn limb from limb by the other pupils.

She was so changed, he did not recognize her.

From *The Hapless Child*.

felonious monks. It is an impious but comic enchiridion of almost all violence, all done, curiously, in a mannered style – he tended to draw people in extended and vaguely balletic postures – and in arch, elegant forms. Violence is the essential Gorey ingredient. It is used in his books with such off-hand wit and inevitability that, having become his signature, if it were suddenly missing, you would begin to worry or at least feel you are being fobbed off by work not of the master's hand.

Then there is the seminal Gorey tale. *The Hapless Child* (1961), in which a diminutive little girl named Charlotte Sophia, as happy and pure as St. Bernadette, swiftly loses her parents (father killed in Africa, mother thereafter declines) and is packed off to a boarding school run by a ferocious-looking dyke. Her classmates are cruel and tear her favorite doll, Hortense, limb from limb. The waif then determines to flee, hoists over the school wall, and wanders – feckless journey or quest, ending either in tragedy or just plain nowhere, had been one of Gorey's major themes from the beginning – the heartless world. Fate keeps on happening. Charlotte is sold to a heartless and drunken brute who feeds the child on "scraps and tap water" and forces her like Bubu of Montparnasse to make artificial flowers, a labor from which, performed by candlelight in a dim cell, she becomes almost blind. Again she flees in her ragged nightie. "Meanwhile," Gorey pitilessly writes, "her father, who was not dead after all, returned home," and then one snowy day he goes motoring – begoggled, comfortably embundled, himself somehow elegantly ghoulish – and runs down (who else?) the little wanderer. But for her alterations, the father does not recognize her as his daughter, and so it ends. Gorey has said that he got the rough idea, although his own plot is different, from a French movie dating from 1905 titled *L'Enfant de Paris*. *The Hapless Child*, one of Gorey's most popular and analyzed books, is, among other things, a wonder in the service of art – a masterpiece of exotic wallpapers.

As to deeper meanings, well, Gorey said, "I generally feel that what you see is what you get, but all those who want to read something into it, poor bunnies, then they can. Half the time, I think, Oh dear, this drawing doesn't mean much. You know, what is it all in aid of? Occasionally, someone will come up to me and say, 'I figured out what your book was about,' and I ask, 'Oh, what?' Then they tell me something completely bizarre. And I'll think," he shrugged, "if that's what you want to see, it's okay by me.'"

Threats (notice a pin-sized creature in each drawing of *The Hapless Child*) are everywhere, mined in every landscape of Gorey, flick-flackering out of

The moon is full: its silver beams
Shine down and give us lovely dreams.

Sing twiddle-ear, sing twaddle-or,
The Wuggly Ump is at the door.

From *The Wuggly Ump*.

the sky – in old gazebos, ornate sofas, flues, orphanages, desolate savannas, winter trees, algae-covered lagoons, snowcapped parapets, cold sheds, endless moors, weather-beaten kiosks, and opera boxes. Innocence seems never out of jeopardy: foundlings with small, weary faces are beaten to death by canes; demireps with eyes rounded by kohl – most women in his books, the elegant ones certainly, are as identifiable for their black eye-liner as Claudia Cardinale – stare hatefully at children; icy-souled coloraturas sneer at penniless clerks in love with them; buzzing insects rape and sacrificially embalm five-year-old girls; guileless ballerinas are snuffed out at the peak of their careers; travelers with gentle hearts disappear forever in dark forbidding hills. The only book of Edward Gorey's with a happy ending is not a "human" book at all but rather one that deals with eight microscopic bugs. As a matter of fact, only one of Gorey's books, *The Wuggly Ump* (1963), was ever specifically published as a children's book. Gorey's entire canon is a long purgatory of muffled hysteria, danger, and strange attrition where endings are invariably inconclusive and always abrupt. All takes place in a calendar of ominous unHalloweens. Ellipses challenge the reader with maddening frequency. Gorey provides no solutions. Matters are simply dropped.

It rather gives one pause to hear that Gorey has gone on record as saying, "I think a lot of my work has to do with reality. I think of my stuff as quite real. I mean, people endlessly nattering on about nothing at all, terrible things happening or nothing happening. I don't know. I'm not a firm believer in cause and effect. Fantasy I've always found a word I don't much care for." Neither did he particularly enjoy the word "macabre" always being applied to him. "It sort of annoys me to be stuck with that, despite all the evidence to the contrary. I don't think that's exactly what I do. I know of course that I do it, but what I'm really doing is something else entirely. It just looks like I'm doing that." He is scouring a deeper reality, I believe he is saying, not simply silly Halloweeniana, in short. "Only a master can allow himself the luxury of seeing things as they are," E. M. Cioran has written, and it well explains how Gorey in expressing his dark vision, his view of reality, may have had such a small, even if passionate, following.

"I don't know, I must see reality different than most people," was a sentence I heard Gorey often repeat. The subject seemed to vex him, although, Lord knows, he surely could not hold fans blameable for assigning him to *le cercle lugubrieux*. The paradox of that protestation always reminded me of a statement that Franz Kafka once made, he who relied so heavily on the letter K for his characters' names: "I find Ks ugly, almost repugnant, and yet I keep on writing them; they must be very characteristic of myself." It is critic Roberto Calasso's observation that "in Kafka's handwriting the letter K plunked downward with a showy swoop the writer detested."

People conjecture that Gorey for the darkness in his books was only living up to his name. It was not quite as bad as "Every human being is a sort of monster, if you get to know them [sic]," as Christina Stead once said. Black humor goes back to the nonsensical wit of André Breton and the Surrealists, Alfred Jarry, and movies like the plotless, subversive *Un Chien Andalou,* but the nightmarish in all its forms has been with us from Aeschylus – murder, suicide, war, barbarism, terminal illness, domestic violence, insanity, nightmare, disease, racism, disability (both physical and mental), corruption, and crime. Gorey even shared with Edgar Allan Poe a dark romanticism, morbidity, fascination with burial, obscurity for obscurity's – and humor's – sake, and even a love of cryptograms which are everywhere in his books. Gorey's in many ways, while cute, is a nose-thumbing attitude, disobedient, rude even.

Edward St. John Gorey ("Ted" to his close friends) was born on February 22, 1925 in Chicago, the son of Edward Leo Gorey and Helen Garvey, who were divorced when he was 11 and remarried when he was 27. Although he is often mistaken for being English, his ancestors were primarily Irish. The Garvey side of his mother's Episcopalian family came from Ireland in the 1850s; his grandfather was a financial executive at Illinois Bell who began his career in the railroads and had a summer home in Winthrop Harbor. Both of Gorey's Catholic paternal grandparents emigrated to Chicago from Ireland in the late 1880s, his grandfather a city "street laborer" for many years before settling the family in Forest Park. Family lore tells of warrior-like Goreys exiled to Europe for fighting with the British government, and Gorey was built like his relatives – tall and thick, with big hands and muscular legs. When I first met him forty years ago he was quite stocky. I'm not saying fat as a potato-chip truck, notice. But he was heavy. He got much thinner toward the end of his life, even gaunt. There cannot be found any short humans in Gorey's work – they are all long limbs, even ungainly, and their torsos are often topped with small bulblike heads. "Hills and valleys," said Gorey about his life – there is an actual town in Ireland, around Wexford, called Gorey – when, after meeting him for the first time in 1972, I got a chance to interview him for an article in *Esquire* magazine a year later in the living room of his cousin's Cape Cod house where he sat, taking toast and chastely sipping a glass of Cranapple juice. I learned that his stepmother from 1936 to 1952 was, curiously enough, Corinna Mura (1909-1965), the exotic-looking, guitar-playing cabaret-singer called Andrea who may be remembered for her vivid rendition of the "La Marseillaise" in the classic movie, *Casablanca* (1942). Born in Texas of Spanish-English-Scottish background, she also appeared in *Call Out the Marines* (1942), *Prisoner of Japan* (1942), *The Gay Senorita* (1945), and the Broadway musical *Mexican Hayride* in 1944-1945. Gorey always told me that his parents encouraged his talents.

I believe that I never, not once, heard Gorey ever speak of his mother, well or ill. Neither did his cousins nor his extended family have anything to say on the subject, when later I made inquiries along those lines. Henry James was always curiously silent about his mother, so was Ho Chi Minh of his, and Charles Dickens, I recall, referred to his mother only once, pointing out that when he was a young lad he wanted to leave Warren's blacking factory where, sticking labels on bottles, working in a window for passersby to see, he was mortified. He sought to leave in order to attend school to better himself, but his mother doggedly insisted that he keep to the job. "I do not write resentfully or angrily: for I know all these things have worked together to make me what I am," Dickens wrote much later in life. "But I never afterwards forgot, I never shall forget, I never can forget, that my mother was warm for my being sent back." It is a mini-phenomenon in lives, I suppose, never mind in letters. Huckleberry Finn seemingly does not have a mother – such a person is never referred to, mentioned not once in the entire novel. Notice how often, by the way, Shakespeare depicts fathers and daughters, but never mothers and daughters, and only occasionally mothers and sons – and *look at them!*

Gorey was an only child, a fact not lost on those who cherish symmetries, especially when one pores over almost any Gorey text and spies out, with alarming recurrence, the little solitaries and tiny, beleaguered waifs with small mole-like faces who invariably scout his karfreitagian world on their own, Gorey being the master of the literary theme academics often refer to as The One Against the Many. And how these lonely figures are invariably sucked dry by leeches, assaulted by bears, smothered by rugs, killed by ennui, run through with awls, or imbedded in ice! Twenty-six hapless children are inventively dispatched in such ways in Gorey's gruesome abecedarian work, *The Gashlycrumb Tinies* or one of the "Three Volumes of Moral Instruction" from *The Vinegar Works* (1963), which, with its drawings set in panels, has since become his most celebrated poster. "For some reason my mission in life is to make everybody as uneasy as possible, because that's what the world is like." Bad behavior, to my mind, always confirmed for Gorey an essential and unavoidable fact of life, proving to his amusement – Stoicism formed from dubious circumspection – not only that this is the way we are, but also in a sense we all live closer to our deficiencies than to our dreams.

I once asked Gorey why the focus of all his books was that particular period when the opulent Edwardian period, "a short-lived wedding party, confined to one brief decade," in the words of Cecil Beaton, segued into the rollicking 1920s, a period that covered the transitional years – one way to remember it – between King Edward's cigars and the smoking of cigarettes. It never failed to amaze me that Gorey showed an almost encyclopedic knowledge of the Edwardian woman. He knew the details. Fine skin was essential. Freckles were shunned. She washed her hair in camomile tea or lemon juice. "If she had fine hair, as Agnes de Mille once noted, she 'gardened' it," he said. "Pinning up one's hair was the equivalent for her of first using lipstick nowadays, and permitting a young man to remove hairpins or combs was the first step toward intimacy, and, unless properly sanctified, it heralded ruin. No Edwardian woman cut her hair short unless she had had typhoid." At the time I happened to be writing a book on the color black. Gorey and I were chatting – from his gray-painted rickety side-porch we sat watching bees sip strawberry blossoms, and I happen to remember it was a May 6th, simply because I never forget the day that Henry David Thoreau passed away – about the distinguished social event known as the "Black Ascot." At the first Ascot racing season after the popular monarch's death, society appeared dressed from head to foot in black. Men wore black silk top hats with morning or frock coats, black waistcoats, black ties, while in their black-gloved hands they carried tightly rolled black umbrellas. Women wore black dresses trimmed with long black fringes, black cartwheel hats, long black gloves, carried black lace parasols, and dainty black shoes. "A lady was known by her dainty foot as well as her voice. Taste spelled quietness, suitability, and hand-sewing," he pointed out, highlighting one of his very own private fascinations. "All Edwardian women could embroider." Gorey was an anglophile, of course, start there. He was also an expert in fashion, pored over histories of fashion, knew lots about period accessories which at a mere glance at any of his books can be confirmed, and would have agreed with Beaton who in *The Glass of Fashion* wrote,

There has been no period in my lifetime more abused, more ridiculed, more hailed as damned, ugly, and wild than the twenties. Perhaps I am rare among my contemporaries in finding that the period was, on the whole, remarkable and vital.

…To me the fashions of the twenties are infinitely alluring.

The era Gorey settled on as an ambient backdrop for his books dealing with the "bright young things" – originally the title of Evelyn Waugh's novel, *Vile Bodies*, but which he changed as he felt the phrase became too clichéd – fit his pen-point to a T. In each little book he wrote over more than half a century we find the *zeitgeist* of the Edwardians and of the Twenties wonderfully evoked, the latter an era when the spirit of masquerade and experiment, daring and even lunacy, reached new heights, when days among the leisured and the advantaged were filled with berrying parties, croquet, daring airplane hops, ingenious treasure hunts, and tennis. Women wore turbans and cloche hats, gypsy skirts and knee-length dresses, head-wraps and skullcaps, outré sashes and bracelets up the arm. It was stylish to affect long cigarette holders and cool to be sporty, wearing "bags" and sweaters. All matriculated in what Beaton called "the *Great Gatsby* era when ladies willed their bodies to look as much like cooked asparagus as possible, taking the form of whatever sofa or chair they sat in." It was the world of Covarrubias cartoons in *Vanity Fair,* the Blackbird revues, witch balls, large Chinese screens, walls *boiseried* in imitation lacquer, and popular songs such as "Button Up Your Overcoat," "You're the Cream in My Coffee" and "I Can't Believe That You're in Love With Me," "When the Choo-Choo Train leaves for Alabam," "What'll I Do," and "Remember." People were going to the theaters to see *Steamboat Willie* (1928), *Pandora's Box* (1929), and *Bunty Pulls the Strings* (1921). Feet were "dogs," bullshit was "piffle," "ducky" meant very good, "voot" was slang for money, "Let's ankle!" indicated going for a walk, and an "Ethel" was an effeminate male.

Young Edward, who was quite precocious and breezed through school, spent most of his time drawing, playing Monopoly ("The game came out when I was about 10 and for months we didn't do anything else"), and reading all the mysteries and the detective novels his parents kept in piles: Ngaio Marsh, Dorothy Sayers, Marjorie Allingham, and particularly Agatha Christie. He *adored* Agatha Christie and was the type of enthusiastic reader of hers, for example, who could talk forever about *The Mysterious Affair at Styles* and speculate forever over who would benefit most from Mrs. Inglethorp's death or ponder forever the significance of Dr. Bauerstein's arrest or discuss into the night the theme of strychnine in that mystery! I mean, fanatical! "When Agatha Christie died, I thought: I can't go on," Gorey went on record as wittily – and exaggeratedly – saying. His good taste was shared by other notables, however. T.S. Eliot once planned a great book on the detective novel, with an entire section devoted to her books. It is also worthy of note that in Roland Barthes's rarefied *Writing Degree Zero*, the only author in English he includes is – Mrs. Christie! Another critic mentions her short story collection, *The Labours of Hercules,* in almost the same breath as Joyce's *Ulysses. (*I can admit to enjoying the play *The Mousetrap* but have to say I could never bring myself to like her books or the dull, creamy readability of her writing. Neither could Raymond Chandler. I tend to agree with the critic Peter Lennon who claimed that "her dialogue is tinnitus to the ear" and that her dénouements were ineffective because "you are not shocked that one of the pieces of cardboard has committed a felony nor do you rejoice that a brown paper bag with a perm has not.") "I also remember reading all the novels of Victor Hugo when I was about eight, which God knows is more than I can do now," Gorey reminisced. "I picked one up a couple of years ago. Chloroform! But I can still remember a Hugo being forcefully removed from my tiny hands when I was about eight, so I could eat my supper." Gorey once mentioned to me that he had composed a handmade book when he was a kid entitled "Hand of Doom," which contained in some kind of running sequence the rebus of a skeleton's hand in various menacing gestures. He also went to the movies a good deal and became obsessed by serials and horror films. He indulged himself reading various genres of books, "loved *The Secret Garden* and the A. A. Milne books," he told Richard Dyer of the *Boston Globe*. "One awful summer my parents sent me to camp, and I spent all my time on the porch reading the Rover Boys. I still reread them now and again. If I liked a book as a child, I assume I would still like it. Both my parents were mystery story addicts, and I read thousands of them myself. Agatha Christie is still my favorite author in all the world; I must have read everything she wrote at least three times." Gorey in fact dedicated one of his funniest books to the mystery writer, a clue-filled but wittily inconclusive parody of her work, *The Awdrey-Gore Legacy* (1972), a small encyclopedia of "mystery" props, types, etc. It is more or less a do-it-yourself handbook on how to write a mystery.

From *The Awdrey-Gore Legacy.*

There are many traits Gorey shared with the mistress of mystery. Aside from the fact that both lived quietly, remotely, and were both ill at ease with unfamiliar people – Agatha Christie's shyness kept her inert at times – both loved gossip, both thought little of the human race, and both pretty much expected the worst of everyone, at least if we can take Miss Jane Marple, a character supposedly based on Christie's grandmother, as a legitimate mouthpiece – in her words she has a mind "like a sink" – but of course highlighting that shared sensibility is the fact that both loved ghoulishness, mayhem, crime, and the joy of delineating delightful malefactors. I think the act of violently dispatching children, in the work of both a common trope, was an anti-social extreme that gave each of them the highest pleasure. Ordeal by innocence, call it. One child is driven off a cliff; one drowns in an apple-bobbing tub. In several novels, morbid children beg to see lifeless corpses. Crime and comedy often went arm in arm with both. Murders incorporating both are gleefully based on children's nursery rhymes! In *Appointment with Death* (1938) what could be more gruesome than the psychotic Mrs. Boynton in that great barrack of a house miles from anywhere preventing her children from making any outside contacts whatsoever and turning them into peculiar, friendless, isolated, even nervy weirdos? I can never read *The Gashlycrumb Tinies* without thinking of their figurative godmother, Agatha Christie.

Gorey attended the distinguished Francis W. Parker private school, skipped several grades – he was obviously precocious from the early drawings, notes, and notebooks that his parents compulsively saved from his youth – graduated, and then from June 1944 to February 1946 whiled away several years in the Army as a Company Clerk stationed at the Dugway Proving Grounds in Utah where they tested mortar and where, years ago, 12,000 sheep were inexplicably gassed to death. After more than twenty-five years of knowing him, I had never once heard a single reference, never mind anecdote, of his Army life, or for that matter, of the state of Utah, although he has gone on record as saying that it was in the Army that he first began writing plays. Such creative work at the time may have served as flight for him, creative voyaging, fugues out of the routine. Edward Gorey, of course, famously did not travel. Only one time did he go abroad – specifically to Scotland, in 1975. "I did not see the monster, to my great regret – the great disappointment of my life," he said, regarding Loch Ness which he toured along with Fair Isle, the Orkneys, the Shetlands, and the Outer Hebrides. From what he always said to me, one place, anyplace, anywhere, seemed just as good as another. "I'm not interested in places from a cultural point of view, thank you. I went for the scenery more than anything else," he once said. "I remember seeing the movie, *I Know Where I'm Going* [1945] with Wendy Hiller and Finlay Currie – a determined, sort of headstrong girl plans to marry someone but gets stranded in a Scottish seacoast town for a week. Petula Clark is in it, folks, which I think might have been her first film. Please, do not *mention* her performance in *Finian's Rainbow* [1968], which is absolutely the worst movie ever made, even though of course I adore Fred Astaire – and, well, I fell in love with Wendy Hiller and the scenery and sort of knew right away I wanted to go there."

He was a man of astonishing extremes. Never traveling, when he was easily one of the most curious people on the planet? Going to the New York City Ballet for 23 seasons from 1956 to 1979 without missing a single one? Living alone for 75 years, and yet writing books so preoccupied with the lives of children (even if it is to dispatch them)? Having read virtually every book that ever was while being a rabid and incontrovertible watcher of TV? Wearing genuine fur coats when he was one of the earth's great animal lovers and a generally devoted conservationist? Exalting the work of director Georges Franju whose savage documentary on the abattoirs of France, *Le Sang des Bêtes* (1949), a gruesome horror, is the locus classicus of horses, cattle, sheep being slaughtered? A reader of sophisticated writers such as Trollope, Tolstoy, and Thackeray who spent days wondering whether the lovely Erica Kane would remain married to David on the television soap-opera *All My Children*? A solitary and habitually remote fellow who was nevertheless also publicly listed in the Cape Cod telephone book? A fellow who loved Bach but listened to the Grateful Dead and on the recommendation of a young nephew went out to buy Phish CDs? A serious artist who much preferred to swap stories about, say, wonderfully dithery Edna Mae Oliver as Hildegarde Withers with her moldy fox-fur in *Murder On A Honeymoon* (1935) rather than discuss his own work, which, as I say, more than anything he absolutely hated to do? Someone who during the darkest years of the Vietnam War or the vileness of Watergate could only find it in his heart of hearts to fret about the fact that the seductress of the silent movies, Rosemary Theby, she of *The Reincarnation of Karma* and *Dice of Destiny* and *The Mystery of 13*, never put her hats on straight? A rabid and intense reader of books who although he had never married could become hugely flummoxed and exercised that with the friend of the narrator's increasing domination by his wife, the Innsmouth sorceress, Asenath Waite, ends up even possessing his body at times in H.P. Lovecraft's remarkably haunting "The Thing on the Doorstep"? This was not a man who did not pursue his own dreams in his own way?

Schooling was no different. He took a Saturday course at the Art Institute of Chicago and attended only one term there after graduating high school – when he switched over to the University of Chicago, he was promptly drafted – which was the entire limit of his training in art. He was primarily self-taught, an astonishing fact when one considers the sophistication of his pen and the magic of his composition.

A point to be underscored is how magnificently Edward Gorey could *draw*. It is noteworthy how little such a thing matters among contemporary artists. I understand Caravaggio didn't draw. Velázquez could not draw. El Greco left approximately one drawing. Thomas Hart Benton said that Jackson Pollock hadn't a clue to drawing. "I agree that the drawing contains distortions," declared a disingenuous Clement Greenberg of a Pollock drawing of a calf, scrambling desperately to try to defend a childlike scrawl. "But it is quite obvious that these are not of a kind due to ineptitude. Notice that there are no errors of proportion or positioning. The distortions are matters of emphasis. I do not see anything grossly inaccurate in the rendering of the torso, and the calf 'jumps' only when you focus on it to the exclusion of everything else; otherwise, it seems a necessary accent." Lee Krasner's drawings are nothing but aggregations of mere sticks. Mark Rothko who began to paint in the Art Students League under Max Weber couldn't draw a pumpkin – he did maps, and his interest even early in life lay less in mimesis than in the so-called expressive "idea." Richard Serra's "drawings" resemble mud spots. "I look at Jeff Koons stuff and I'm appalled," said rocker Patti Smith. "Somebody like Jeff Koons I think is just litter upon the earth, I look at his stuff and I'm appalled." On the other hand, "drawing has never been compulsory for genius," states James Fenton in his book of essays on art and artists, *Leonardo's Nephew*, where he points out that Jasper Johns always made it his practice to paint first, draw later. That may be the case – I know that the genius Andrew Wyeth is today even blasphemously mocked for his realistic drawings and paintings, mostly by fools jealous of his almost unparalleled brilliance – but Gorey's ability along these lines were awesome.

Harvard followed: Gorey entered in 1946 and took his B.A. in 1950, having concentrated in French ("I figured nothing in the curriculum would advance my career, so why not take French?"); for two and a half years his roommate was the late poet Frank O'Hara, whose poetry he found fairly

One of young Gorey's very first posters, drawn at Harvard, 1952.

unmemorable, or so he once mentioned to me. Gorey did a lot of drawing in college, doing various things for the *Harvard Advocate* and illustrating several books of poetry, most notably those of psychiatrist and poet Merrill Moore and Medford, Mass. poet John Ciardi, whose courses in creative writing he and his friends all took at Harvard. He stuck around Boston until January 1953, working part-time in a bookstore for a while and composing witty limericks that he would later parlay into his second book, *The Listing Attic* (1954). He also began fooling around with the Poets' Theater in the summer of 1949, illustrating sets and drawing posters – indeed, one of my personal treasures, which I found in an antique market in the 1970s in western Massachusetts, is an original poster, signed "EG," that Gorey designed and drew for the Poets' Theater, dated March 10, 1952, of Dylan Thomas reading from *King Lear* as well as his own poetry ("admission $1.00"). He even wrote and directed plays, a fascination that continued to his death, quite passionately and quite devotedly, with the puppet plays which he scripted, organized, and directed on Cape Cod more or less annually during the summer months. I would love to have read one particular play that he wrote after college for the Poets' Theater in 1952, part of an evening's entertainment that quite prefigured his later work. It was called *The Teddy Bear: a Sinister Play*, and in it a stuffed Teddy bear strangles infants while his fat, dopey parents gamble and play cards. "There was a marvelous group of fascinating and creative people involved with the Poets' Theater," Gorey once explained. "A great deal of excitement in the air, with faculty, graduates, undergraduates. It was goofy amateur theater where we all did very arty plays and came up with all sorts of ideas and projects. 'Ooooh, goody,' we'd say, devising something or other. And then 'Oh, God, what was that all about?' as we watched it sink without a trace."

Gorey took quite a while before he saw any clear direction to his life's work. In 1998, he told the Boston *Globe*, "I wanted to have my own bookstore until I worked in one. Then I thought I'd be a librarian until I met some crazy ones. I hoped to get into publishing, but, at 28, my parents were still helping me out. Which wasn't good at all."

A momentary reflection. I do not believe in all the years I knew him, walked through the shadowy Gorey world of attrition and asynartesia, that I heard with more frequency – applied with black glee to any and all undertakings, a plan, a project, a pet dream – his universally wistful comment (often made with a bead-like stare at the horizon), about any project he took up, "It will disappear like the *neiges d'antan*."

And then in 1953 after some friends who worked at Doubleday in New York had helped Gorey find a job with that publisher, he moved permanently to New York City, where he took an apartment in a 19th century townhouse and began working in the design department with Anchor Books illustrating book jackets of rereleased out-of-print classics, such as Chaucer's *Troilus and Cressida*, Franz Kafka's *Amerika,* Mikhail Lermontov's *A Hero of Our Time*, Nikolai V. Gogol's *Tales of Good and Evil,* Joseph Conrad's *The Secret Agent,* and so forth. He drew covers for Doubleday for seven years. His first two books, brought out by the now-defunct publishers Duell, Sloan & Pearce, *The Unstrung Harp* (1953) and *The Listing Attic* (1954), now almost impossible to find in first editions – it was Dr. Merrill Moore, a Boston psychiatrist and a member of the Fugitive group of poets, who introduced Gorey to Duell, Sloan, and Pearce – a wistful Gorey later recalled seeing being sold at one point in great remainder-piles on 42nd Street for 19 cents each. (How ironic and yet fitting that on that very same Broadway his set-designs for *Dracula*, full proscenium sets all black-and-white, each touched with only a single spot of red, would win a Tony Award in 1978!) A true first-edition of *The Fantod Pack,* unauthorized and pirated from a 1966 issue of *Esquire* magazine, 22 tarot-type cards, fluorescent green cardstock printed in purple, wrapped in a printed yellow sheet with a printed blue sheet wrapped around them, presently sells for $4500. *The Eclectic Abecedarium,* one of 100 signed copies hand-colored by Gorey comprising a deluxe grouping of a printing of 400, sells for $2500. His *Story for Sara: What Happened to a Little Girl*, written by the witty homophonist Alphonse Allais (1854-1905) – one of his ingenious couplets in holorhymic verse-form goes:

> *par les bois du djinn où s'entasse de l'effroi*
> *Parle et bois du gin ou cent tasses de lait froid*

sells for $1850. Generally freelancing about with his weird little drawings, he was unable to flog to any publisher a first book he had by then finished called *The Beastly Baby* – no publisher would go near it – which was eventually released in 1962. "Nobody would touch my book proposals. So I said to hell with it," he explained with a shrug, "and published them myself under my own imprint, the Fantod Press. I did all of the work myself, the drawings, the texts in hand lettering, the layout, the covers. Most were printed in editions of about 200." I have seen *The Beastly Baby*, probably Gorey's rarest book, selling

Its hands were both left ones.

Its nose was beaky, and appeared to be considerably older than the rest of it.

Its tiny eyes were surrounded by large black rings due to fatigue, for its guilty conscience hardly <u>ever</u> allowed it to sleep.

It was usually damp and sticky for it wept a great deal. It was consumed by self-pity, which in this case was perfectly justified.

From *The Beastly Baby.*

(unsigned) for about $800 per copy and with the rare book/first edition trolls, the bottom-feeders of the book-selling world, even higher prices than that. This tiny black comedy is one of the most calmly irreverent and horrific pieces I have ever read. After publication, he received copies of it in the mail from outraged mothers, ripped to shreds, the exact situation that Thomas Hardy faced after the publication of his, at the time, highly controversial novel, *Jude the Obscure,* with puritans in high dudgeon ripping up the book, which made him quit writing novels for the last thirty years of his life. Fans, interviewers, people of all sorts have asked Edward Gorey for fifty years why it was that he hated children. His memorable – and, I believe, now celebrated – answer? "I don't know any children."

His perspective on suffering, Aristotelian in concept, had to do with the kind of catharsis we read about in the *Poetics.* The slant was satire, the pungent if raw criticism mounted against human behavior. A gruesome baby in *The Beastly Baby* explodes like a wet balloon in mid-air! Rapscallions had hijacked suffering into sentimentality, I think he felt. In his irreverence Gorey was not the Jeroboam of his age, however, leading us all into sin. He was classically disinterested. His was not *saeva indignatio,* nothing like it, merely the kind of warring wit, the same vitalizing if vicious send up we find in Twain mocking the ritualistic Victorian attitude toward death with his parody poem, "The Ode to Stephen Dowling Bots" in *Adventures of Huckleberry Finn.* "Don't let your mind be disabled by excessive sympathy," I remember reading the aged George Bernard Shaw confided to a neighbor during the Blitz of Britain. "When things look very black, it is well to remember that public evils are not millionfold evils. What you yourself can suffer is the utmost that can be suffered on earth." He went on,

> *If you starve to death, you experience all the starvation that has ever been or ever can be. If ten thousand others starve with you, their suffering is not increased by a single pang; their share in your fate does not make you ten thousand times as hungry nor prolong your suffering ten thousand times. You should not therefore be oppressed by the frightful sum of human suffering. There is no sum. Two lean women are not twice as lean as one nor two fat women twice as fat as one. Poverty and pain are not cumulative, and you must not let your spirit be crushed by the fancy that it is. If you can stand the suffering of one person, you can fortify yourself with the reflection that the suffering of millions is no worse.*

"When I was 12, I read a book called *A High Wind in Jamaica* by Richard Hughes. In it good-natured pirates rescue some kids from a hurricane. But in the end the kids are responsible for having the pirates hanged. That," said Gorey, working that voice that was always simultaneously both ironic and informed, "killed the myth about innocent children for me. It was the sort of book you never forget, and you never feel the same because of it. I didn't need *Lord of the Flies* as a paradigm." He was right, of course. Schoolyards throughout the country are the national grids of some of the worst cruelty and nastiest torture imaginable. Moronic bullies had picked on both the two Columbine High School shooters for years, so badly that in the process of killing all of those innocent students they were willing to die themselves. Why was the bullying never discussed? It has remained to this day the most ignored aspect of that murderous story – and it goes on in every school and schoolyard in every state in the country *still!* As poet Marianne Moore wrote, "What is our innocence,/What is our guilt? All are/naked, none is safe."

Other books with which Gorey had trouble were *The Bug Book* (1959), because the villain was black – "We got some flak about that," said Gorey, "which I thought was ridiculous beyond belief," – and *The Loathsome Couple* (1977), a tale based on the notorious Moors Murder Case in Yorkshire, England where depraved Ian Brady and Myra Hindley murdered youngsters and recorded their voices, and, said Gorey, "admittedly comes as close to anything as wildly unpleasant as I have done – various book shops sent it back." It was not a comedy to him, nevertheless. Writing it was a grim task. "That [murder spree] upset me dreadfully, even after years of reading crime stories." It was in every detail a story that he felt compelled to write and to illustrate and so he did. There is a line in Gorky's *My Universities* – after an attempt at suicide, at 19, in December 1887, he travelled on foot across the Russian Empire for five years, changing jobs and accumulating impressions used later in his writing – that applies here: "I noticed – how many times? – that everything unusual and phantastical, however far from the truth it might be – appeals to people much more than serious stories of actual life."

The years in Cambridge were a period during which Gorey started "an endless number of novels," now, alas, all jettisoned. He worked for Adlai Stevenson in 1952 in Boston, "became unstrung by it all," as he put it, and after that experience took up his palette and shuffled off. Politics always bored Gorey. Typically, however, he was well versed on the subject. "We were all very much against Jack Kennedy because as a senator he refused to stump for Stevenson. I voted one time, for Stevenson in 1952." But the fact of the matter is Gorey was always completely alert as to which politician was running and why. I have alluded to the poet-physician Merrill Moore (1903-1957) and how he helped Gorey when he was younger. It was the eccentric Moore – he would walk barefoot through Boston, wearing a full suit, to attend hospital and academic meetings, because he "liked the feel of grass in his toes" – who put the young Robert Lowell in contact with the literary world including Ford Madox Ford, Allen Tate and John Crowe Ransom, and who also encouraged Lowell to become a student of Ransom after Lowell's sudden violent break with his own family and departure from Harvard. Moore also advised his close friend Robert Frost on the medical treatment of two of his troubled children. After World War II, Moore played a key behind-the-scenes role in the fascist controversy with Ezra Pound, as a member of a group of literary men who saw to it that the modernist icon escaped a treason trial for his radio propaganda in support of Mussolini. Moore was a close friend of one of the psychiatrists on a diagnostic panel that found Pound unfit to stand trial. Merrill Moore was a compulsive writer of sonnets – one estimate has it that he wrote as many as 50,000 of them! – and to my mind some of Edward Gorey's most memorable illustrations were done for Moore's books, notably *Illegitimate Sonnets*; *Case Record from a Sonnetorium*; *Clinical Sonnets*; and *More Clinical Sonnets,* all featuring that odd, chart-holding, capybara-headed creature in a physician's smock who with his fixated stare looked quite mad. From all reports Gorey in his Harvard years showed with a kind of bold insouciance as much of a "flambeaued manner," to use a Wallace Stevens phrase, as he would later, facing his life with the strongly-held if defensive belief, Stevens here again, that living a life of imagination is the richest and most productive way to evade "the world without imagination." A voracious reader, moviegoer, TV-watcher, and culture maven, Gorey who burned with a "hard, gem-like flame" had to have a constant stream of information coming in, of every stripe. He needed to know everything. He was both a dreamer and a realist. He *felt* things. He was an aesthetician. People, in a social sense, tended to get in the way of this. He did have close friends, insofar as people like Gorey have friends, but most people in his case, I am fully convinced, were made – kept as – acquaintances. Did he compartmentalize? I was told by several good folk who, having attended his Memorial Service (I myself could not bear to attend), were struck by how many people who claimed to be his best friend did not know each other. Actress Julie Harris, a good friend, read *The Osbick Bird*.

He was paradoxical about his fellow man: He held people at bay on the one hand, simply because he was so obliging and generous, on the other, that he checked himself to forfend the possibility of being usurped, simply because he loved to talk, and he was filled with opinions on every subject, and on a very happy afternoon with the sun out when he was rested he could be even almost Pickwickian. He refused to take himself seriously and in a way called to mind for me the lines in Wallace Stevens's poem, "A High-Toned Old Christian Woman," a brief didactic and satirical poem, where the real artists,

> *Your disaffected flagellants, well-stuffed,*
> *Smacking their muzzy bellies in parade,*
> *Proud of such novelties of the sublime,*
> *Such tink and tank and tunk-a-tunk-tunk,*
> *May, merely may, madame, whip from themselves*
> *A jovial hullabaloo among the spheres.*

Edward Gorey was tall, sported a white beard, and had a glittering eye, with often the wee trace of a smile, but his face was gaunt, a bit saturnine, and often studiously uncertain, his mien suggesting the somewhat endungeoned, rather like a saint who lives on pulses, lentil soup, and alarming news. He was very informal and had a long-standing reputation, especially during the years he lived in New York City, for appearing in heavy raccoon coats, tennis shoes, and lots of arty iron jewelry, most of which eventually gave way later in life in terms of focus to the plethora of iron rings and brass pendants that he began to wear and that always clinked and chimed whenever he expressively flung out his hands to talk. (On given days, Gorey, like the eccentric Edith Sitwell and drummer Ringo Starr, to name but two, might have worn as many as ten rings. "It's theatrical! It hurts no one," was the late Sammy Davis, Jr.'s comment on the amount of hefty rocks he wore.) Gorey was balding and spoke with a rather fey tone, heavily sibilant, and his voice, mirthful almost always among friends, could border on glee when he was enthusiastic or excited. He invariably stood in the naturalistic stance known as *contrapposto,* hand on hip, like Gainsborough's *The Blue Boy* or Donatello's *David* but at times he would appear almost in balletic "turn out" or fully cross-legged – a gay icon – in exaggerated pose.

When he became reflective about something, pondering, say, a question you asked, he had a way of clenching his hand and pressing it to his mouth, looking into the far distance as if the answer had just flown away. He had the Celtic tendency to express affection disguised as abuse or gentle mockery. Cynicism might have muffled sadness for him, and, who knows, jollity may have done the same. From all I saw he discounted disappointment by anticipating it. His were hemlocks – to paraphrase Wallace Stevens – "in which the sun could only fumble," and if he wrote "of ourselves and of our origins,/In ghostlier demarcations, keener sounds," Stevens again in "The Idea of Order at Key West," it was because that was quite the way he saw the world, through a glass darkly, when he was looking at all.

When he was not petting a cat, dramatic gestures, along with heavy sighs or moans, almost always accompanied his highly various conversation. He would chatter on with a kind of fey, self-amused intolerance of things, squawking through a very pronounced sibilance in moments of both delight and exasperation with his own slang expressions, like "Not on your tin-type!" "Snuggy-poos, *desist*!" – when addressing his cats – "Talk about loopy!" "What is that blather about?" He would break into almost Japanese fits of giggling. Whenever I went into one of my rants on whatever subject and was on a roll, he would usually sit there without saying a word, amused, to hear me out, then ask, "Now shall we have a rum shrub?" He himself was constantly coming out with neo–Firbankian remarks like, "I'm a great one for drift" and "Oh please don't, I would rather be smothered in bunny fur!" and "The kind of things I'm attracted to are nonchalant" and "I adore finials" and "Frankly, one of the great deprivations of my life is that I could never quite learn to do papier-mâché correctly." "Spiffy," "icky," "zippy" and "bunty" were popular adjectives with him. Or "zingy." An object to him requiring a description was often "twee" or "kitten cute" or a "fright." "Jeepers!" he would exclaim. "Oh dear" was a favorite ecphonesis of his, almost always used as a response – never without sarcasm or understatement – to bad taste (someone else's). "To die for" was one of his pet verbal items, an expression I particularly loathe, pagan, stupid, vulgar, even blasphemous. He loved uttering oddballisms. "I have not felt that the world was in tune, frankly, since Anne Baxter divorced John Hodiak!" he'd say. Or "Barbara Walters, I'm afraid, belongs to the communion of kitsch, rather than the art of communication." Or "Have you the feeling, when Pavarotti is singing, he is also inflating?" Or "*Bowanga! Bowanga!* is the definitive jungle movie – unless you care to make a case for *Wild Women of Wongo*." For the amusement of others and of course his own, he would often intersperse his conversation with French terms. "*Êtes-vous prêt*, Alexander dear, to hear that I would not pick up that novel again – with *tongs*?" "Oh please, the French have been proving for centuries that they have the worst taste of *absolument* everybody!" "*Quel tabernacle*, that gazebo!"

Was it from reading Henry James that he became so fond of sprinkling his sentences with French phrases? Or Holly Golightly? He could be affected. It was all harmlessly whimsical. On a given day, the adjective "terribly" was over-employed, never without a hand-flap and the accompanying clank of the many rings he wore, as I say. He cherished the artistic. He also admired the perverse, the capricious, the rare, the *sentiment de luxe*. I suspect he knew that all memorable personalities are excessive to a degree, and his own excesses were perfectly natural to him. I found something innocent in the way he surrendered to his own dreams without compromising himself to impress – or court – the world. What if poses were assumed? I was and am often mildly intrigued by what is being said by men who wear pendants, people like Rod Steiger, Elton John, Prince, and Edward Gorey, who favored iron crosses. Does the wearer secretly yearn to be a bishop? But he created his own reveries, and if you found him wearing strange new ear-rings or came across in his house a shallow bowl floating with dried pea-colored poppy heads stippled in gold paint or heard him suddenly singing Noël Coward's "I've Been to a Marvelous Party," you were only too happy to encounter a person following his own bliss.

I have mentioned rings. What was being said with his wearing so many so often? I mean, he was forested with them. Lush. Almost Solomonic in the traipsing kingship of clank! Who would deny an announcement was being made? After all, a ring is symbolic of something, mainly a commitment, at least as the bourgeois world understands it. Going steady. College. Engagement. Marriage. Or was it preening, a real plea for an aesthetic? Most of the rings he wore were iron, had to be uncomfortable to a degree. I suggest it was an attempt at wanting to *belong*. Even badly, one may say. "This represents…!" An identity-assertion, if not a serious existence-assertion. But what was the nature of that identity? It may be argued that Gorey in his dress (mink coat, rings, sneakers – always plimsoll types, etc.) was on the other hand constantly asserting, "I am not at all like you," and needless to say those large but not valuable rings he wore like knuckledusters were arguably in that mode, sometimes two *on a finger,* in this case to call attention to his hands (as a ring inevitably does), as power symbols, another affectation, as another symbol of difference. Could it have been that he was obsessed not so much with the wish to show himself a person of consequence as much as "I am not just an ordinary man"? Imagine for a moment his meeting *another* person in a mink coat and sneakers, dangling earrings, wearing a pile of rings! Yet the event is almost unimaginable and surely could never have happened. The fact of the matter is that in private he wore not only conventional clothes but actually dressed down, old rumpled shirts, frayed denim shorts, especially when he was working, feverishly, almost like a drudge. One may say his dressing-up was a way of subverting that private self. So was it that he wished to be seen and not understood but wanted to confuse the stranger with the display of his fetish objects (African witch doctors also adopt such weird costumes, even to the rings)? "I am not you" extended to books and movies, no? One would praise a good movie, as my brother Paul once did with Nicolas Roeg's *Don't Look Now,* when Gorey mocked and said, "That silly little dwarf in the red hat!" and then praised *Dallas* – "Don't you adore Barbara Bel Geddes as Miss Ellie?" – a direct quote! By no means is it above or beyond a complicated person to need to be both, public and private, at one time ornamented, at another time not. Maybe that was just another excess.

Gorey was forever amused by the excesses and lunacies of this world, which he greeted with surprised laughter, not scorn. Well, sometimes scorn. In a way, he was something of an innocent and had no real personal vitriol. He could not fix things and often did not know the way to or from. Every movie he hated was incontestably "*the* worst movie ever made," every pain-in the-ass "absolutely the worst person inhabiting this planet." He would often dismiss someone off-handedly, darkly muttering, "Of that person, the less said the better." My brother Paul who did not know him well but who is highly perceptive suggested to me that he was "immature." Paul told me, "He is so elusive, and even in conversation he always deflected ('Don't you love Alexis Carrington in *Dynasty*?'). Can his work be analyzed?

Top photo: EG with his cousins on Sandy Neck Beach, Cape Cod.

Bottom photo: EG (in striped shirt) with cousins and a friend at beach in Barnstable Harbor, Cape Cod.

I have tried and failed to make sense of much of it, and yet it is enjoyable for the complexity of manner and the arch tone; but is there a point other than amusement?" Gorey was not immature, although he could be childish, absurdly silly even – he often let his geek flag fly – but rather a truly exquisite illustrator as well as a man who was also complex, insightful, softly kind, very strange, oblique, arrogant rarely except maybe regarding feelings of guilt, an artist occasionally hostile, anti-social, rebellious, highly individual, sometimes unforgiving, and occasionally truly profound.

He tended not to answer letters or even return telephone calls. He rarely sent thank-you notes. It did not seem to occur to him, for all of his busyness and the way his days were cramful, perhaps – although I tend not to accept that, he simply didn't *want* to – that this was discourteous. I don't think he wrote many letters, or in fact even wrote letters at all, certainly not toward the latter part of his life, and of course he died before the personal computer became a way of life. (He did buy a Macintosh in the last year of his life but maybe looked at it twice). "One could say," Franz Kafka complained, "that all misfortunes in my life stem from letters…I have hardly ever been deceived by people, but letters have deceived me without fail…not other people's letters, but my own." I would venture to say that of his brunt-bearing that summed it up on letters.

> Thanks ever so for the neat skull.
> Did you knock at the door?
> My cats must have all been more
> than usually comatose....
>
> EG.

A personal note from Gorey to the author.

Very often he would not answer his door. Maddeningly, he was almost impossible to reach by attempts at knocking when he was so inclined. His doors lacked knobs, and I am convinced they were intentionally left that way; you were never quite certain that the doorbell was audible within, and so one was forced to rap on the glass. "I am not here," Ken Morton, Gorey's much younger first cousin once removed, remembers him shouting whenever the telephone rang. (Ted and Ken's mother were first cousins – Ted's mother and Ken's grandfather were siblings.) Presently a docent at the Gorey House and an amazing fellow in his own right who literally grew up with the man, Ken who grew up spending much time at that seaside house on Millway often heard the ring of that telephone, an instrument, let us say, not particularly suited to Mr. Gorey's particular brand of declamation. (The secret code to reach Gorey – one that he gave out to certain friends – was to call him, let it ring once, hang up, then call back, and he would almost always answer.) The outgoing message on his answering machine was not so much cold as just emotionally dead, the flat under-modulated sound of a robot, and when by some miracle he did personally answer the telephone it was with the flattest, most lugubrious "hello" you have ever heard. Society for him meant a few friends, nothing more. He did not shmooze, to use a hideous Yiddishism. No, he was not Perle Mesta, nor was meant to be. No matter how much a local "must-get" he was among the arty-farty-party set on Cape Cod, he obliged very few. But he was frankly a failure as a recluse, for he openly grocery shopped, walked around flea markets, lunched out daily, mind you, almost always in the same restaurant – I myself cannot stand going out to eat at noon and would rather be shot dead than do it in the same *place* every day – and went trotting off to the movies pretty much every night. "I am very hidebound," he told virtually every interviewer. "I do the same thing over and over. I tend to go to pieces if my routine is broken."

He was up and about, in short. I am convinced that he wanted and even needed attention more then he would ever have admitted and with his highly visible self he putt-putted about for years with his high profile, long scarf, "Ogdred" license plate, and big white sneakers. From the beginning, of course, he artistically insinuated himself into his work – that New Testament beard, that phalanx of iron rings, that fur-coated fellow in sneakers – as a sort of alter-ego. Or *was* that him? "It's a kind of this-is-me-but-it's-not-me thing," he once explained to me, a matter, needless to say, of which every artist, writer or painter, has a full understanding. While he could be convivial, however, he was decidedly not gregarious, mainly because he was always self-booked for the day, drawing, writing, feeding cats, working on a particular assignment, maybe visiting a bookshop, and then of course in the afternoon watching soap operas on television. "There are scads of things I have to see," he would say, "and I'm running way behind."

B

ut then again why should he have answered doors or phones? To appease the herd, the *hoi polloi,* the guttercats and vulgarians of Glickfair, as in *What Makes Sammy Run?* Let's face it, most people are bores and tiresome beyond words, and Gorey had a low threshold for the usual, the flat, the common, the typical, and the predictable. There was that, but he was also curiously diffident. At times it struck me that a certain self-consciousness warred against his high profile appearance which he may have maintained, I don't know, as a corrective or balance to a milquetoastian side. He had few illusions about his own appearance – "Myself the only kangaroo among the beauty," wrote Emily Dickinson – his own goals, his own ambitions, his own fame. I have always felt that the opinion he held of his own great talent and qualities was far, far lower than objectivity warranted. When I had the chance to see a magnificent poster he had just finished, I asked, "Don't you admire it?" He gave a casual shrug. I could not believe it. "Don't you admire your work?" "For about 20 minutes," he replied, dryly. He would talk volubly, but he was also circumspect or at least fundamentally reticent. He liked silence. He valued time. He was methodical. He had custody of himself. Above all, he *enjoyed* being alone, something dim, unoriginal, lazy, and uncreative people pathetically often have not a clue about.

He was reclusive yet available, in neither extreme like the Peter Cook whom Alan Bennett comically writes about who once appeared in a sketch in which, dressed as Greta Garbo, he was filmed touring the London streets in a sleek, open-topped limousine shouting through a megaphone, "I want to be alone."

Gorey did not want someone bothering him. His was not the realm where "if I love-a you and love-a you true and if you-a love-a me, one live as two, two live as one, under the bamboo tree." In a sense, he was even spoiled, culture-hunting, needing to know, shopping for himself, thinking interminably of scenes for which to supply his pen. He was never not busy. He flourished, feeding his own needs and truly savored "the time when he stood alone, /When to be and delight to be seemed to be one," as Wallace

Stevens put it in *Ideas of Order*. His idea of order was living alone. He followed
E.E. Cummings's math, "One's not half two. Its two are halves of one," and
lived in a "sunlight of oneness." There is one theory that holds narcissism to
be the central psychological trope for homosexuality, a life seeking reflections.

What did drag Gorey out of the house other than to eat or see a movie was
basically to do errands. To go to yard sales. Or food shopping. Basic needs. If
he had had a servant or two, I believe no one would have actually *ever* seen
the man. Regarding Gorey, I often thought of the poignancy of Henry James's
remark, "The point from which I set out was, I think, the essential loneliness
of my life." I tend to feel that is the case, one way or another, in the lives of
all true artists. What connected Gorey to the world, in my opinion, was that
he could not tolerate being cut off from information. He needed to absorb
everything – half the time, the less worthwhile the better. He needed to *know*.
Curiously, he was often fascinated by the very things that he abhorred. It is
an important fact to know about him, or about any artist. He had exquisite
taste, but he could descend and was ruled as much by his aversions. He had
faith in almost nothing and sort of loved it. He was not an actual misanthrope
but rather congenitally irreverent, bordering on the hopelessly cynical, and an
infusion of the world's daily idiocies and lunacies and crudities and excesses
by way of television or newspapers may have been required viewing for him,
allowing him a sort of grim buoyancy perhaps. He nevertheless drew lines,
refusing to be co-opted, and he joined nothing. Community he abhorred. He
stayed aloof. As the Brits say, he was not clubbable.

I love his tidy autograph. I believe his signature warrants further study.
It is, if you squint, not unlike the distinctive hand-lettering, a serified
regular face, kerned by hand, commonly used in many of his hand-
lettered books such as *The Blue Aspic* or *The Beastly Baby* or *The Lavender
Leotard* or *The Recently Deflowered Girl* or *The Wuggly Ump*. (Both cats
and bats became something of symbols for him. Just as J.M. Whistler
signed his work with a butterfly, and Eduardo Galeano with a little pig,
Gorey at one time doodled a bat or a cat into many drawings.) His was
a signature that resembled that of the eccentric novelist, Frederick Rolfe
(Baron Corvo), the saintly madman. Was he proud or sensitive about
his name? Who can say? Maybe he was boastful. I have been told that
handwriting-analysis with virtually any example on paper can give you up
to 300 character-attributes of a person. What would a graphologist say of
Gorey's? It is the calligraphy of an artist's, clearly, embellished, floral even,

THE GASHLYCRUMB TINIES

From *The Gashlycrumb Tinies.*

a swipe showing a need to be center of attention, or so I would guess. It is clearly that of someone with intellect, style, a sharp and sensitive mind, someone possibly too dependent to be accommodating or too educated to be second-guessed or possibly a person difficult to understand. Barbs possibly hint at intolerance. It is that of someone who had a sharp eye for experience, failing which, to my mind, no amount of "style" was worth the trouble. In the world of Goreyography, a Gorey serif font from "True Type," one based on Gorey's distinctive hand-lettering – "free for all noncommercial use," according to the Internet – has been created by a Mr. Damien Hess, who claims, "I made this because I was looking for it and couldn't find it."

Fans he tolerated, there were many, but he always obliged them. "We've got a 'customer,'" I have heard him say with a sing-song lilt on the first syllable whenever a fan, an avid reader, or some Gorey groupie or other would appear on his front porch or stop to stand in front of his house. I later learned it was the term Garbo used regarding her own importunate movie fans. A notably avid contingent of Gorey followers are Goth people, dressed in full black, with tats, black boots and exotic hair-cuts. Siobhan Magnus, an *American Idol* TV contestant in 2010, sports on her right arm a tattoo of the dramatic skullman-and-umbrella from *The Gashlycrumb Tinies*. A pretty young woman once came up to him (but this happened quite often) and, gushing, nervously said, "Mr. Gorey, I love your books and honestly have to say that you have changed my life." To which he replied, looking away – mordantly but of course trying to amuse her – "I'm sorry for that. I do hope you'll forgive me." As Alan Bennett has pointed out, not all writers or artists have fans, as opposed to readers. While W. Somerset Maugham has readers, James Joyce has fans. Katherine Mansfield has readers, Jane Austen has fans. Garry Trudeau has readers, Charles Schulz has fans, and so on. Edward Gorey quite pronouncedly has fans. With his work, he created a subculture of sorts, an exclusive, even clubby, self-selected following in the form of dedicated pursuivants (young women I have noticed seem to be the most susceptible) who tend not only to insert themselves into the milieu of his books and characters – Hallowe'en night has become in a few select places for a few select souls a big Gorey occasion – but who often simply telephoned him from faraway places to introduce themselves just to talk. I would see him wobble off to the back of his house to check if he had a scheduled commitment and groan.

A person hell-bent on himself is often a curmudgeon. Dr. Sam Johnson. Voltaire. Mark Twain. H.H. Munro. Frederic Rolfe. Philip Larkin. George Bernard Shaw. Redd Foxx. St. Paul himself was not free of denunciation and name-calling or in fact of recurrent contempt for his rivals and opponents, and he often gives way to unrelieved invective. He speaks with scorn, even derision, of such matters as circumcision (Phil. 3:2) and wishes that advocates of it would fully mutilate themselves (Gal. 5:12) See also Gal. 1:7-8; Phil. 1:15-16 and 3:18-19; 2 Cor. 2:17 and 11:12-15; and Rom. 16:18.

Although Gorey granted interviews, more in fact than any celebrity I know, I suspect he did not really enjoy them. Is it that he was simply too polite to refuse them? Or possibly too diffident to want to ponder it? Who knows? It was only one of a thousand contradictions about the man. He didn't try very hard when he was doing an interview. I think he found it tiresome to repeat things – "Most interviewers don't ask me the questions they should ask me," he once remarked to Clifford Ross – but I do not believe he was introspective in ways that he wanted others to hear about. It seems to me that at bottom he really did not want to explain himself, sometimes even wanted to present himself as mysterious, which is why he often appeared so evasive and so unstrung. Maybe he felt he was wasting time. Words as such "failed" for Gorey in the same way they did for, say, William Faulkner and Samuel Beckett; words are poor, inexact and ineffective commodities, missing the mark and creating mischief, and while they are all we have, he mistrusted them as working toward any real solution. Who knows, perhaps he mistrusted himself using them. I am convinced that Gorey's work had as much to do with language as anything else – the dilemma of language, the ambiguities of language, the inexactitude of language, its enigmas, its dead ends, its comic possibilities, its playfulness. I have no doubt that one day doctoral dissertations on that man will be written, things like "Edward Gorey and Jacques Derrida: The Text of the Cartoon," and "Semiotics in Goreyland" and "The Lexical Weltanschauung of Edward Gorey." "The trouble with interviews," Gorey once quite seriously remarked, "is that you say the same things so often you end up believing them."

"I hate being characterized," he once complained to Richard Dyer on the subject of his being seen as notoriously withdrawn or as a person so elliptical in his art. I think he was suspicious of easy resolution, anywhere, anyway, anyhow. Nor was he comfortable being pegged in an oversimplified way as a sort of Gothic cartoon. "I don't like to read about the 'Gorey details' and that kind of thing. [Dung in medieval times, interestingly enough, was often referred to as *gore*, a meaning now obsolete, that originally signified filth and slime, with its second definition being blood.] Who would deny that for any truly intelligent human being there is a comfort in ambiguity? Is not narrow definition made for the churl and the chump? "I admire work that is neither one thing nor the other, really," he said. "All the things you can talk about in anyone's work are the things that are least important. It's like the ballet. You can describe all the externals of a performance – everything, in fact, but what really constitutes its core. Explaining something makes it go away, so to speak; what's important is what's left after you have explained everything else. Ideally, if anything were good, it would be indescribable. What's the core of Mozart or of Balanchine? That's why I think Henry James is nonexistent. The longer he goes on, the more he explains, there is nothing left."

Gorey was resolutely an individual. He was one of only two or three people I know who every minute of the day, year and year out, simply all the time, did exactly what he wanted. It was not his way to hearken to systematically-argued views. He lived according to his tastes, unfettered by second-hand opinions. He listened to no set call and shunned any imbruing advice, even if helpful, he did not seek out, reminding me somewhat of what Robert Frost once grumpily snapped at an over-solicitous nurse as he proceeded to walk out of a hospital, "I've lived a life of decisions, not indecisions, not even consulting anyone." His restless curiosity did not extend that far. Not a chance. On the other hand, he became easily distracted. "I will do practically anything rather than sit down and work. With the slightest reason to leave the house, I am gone. In New York, for example, once I get out the door, the day is shot. It is fatal. Whereas on the Cape, if I should go outside, I usually get right back in. I don't know anybody down here, for one thing, except during summer. But don't get me wrong, kiddo" – a favorite noun of his, which was never actually directed at anyone in particular or, to put it more accurately, was probably directed at everybody – "anonymity is a blessing. When all my relatives are here, I get a certain amount of steam up. I usually do the cooking. I can cook pretty much anything, however complicated, if no one is particularly fussy and when it's all over with it doesn't have to look pretty. I do not 'do' presentation, thank you. Or let's say I can, but *danke schön*, no thanks." I always used to tell him to buy the best lobsters, never "soft-shells" or "infirms" and that Maine lobstermen always steam their lobsters in a very small amount of sea-water, 17 minutes for the average size (1 ½ lbs.) – food for some reason became a fascinating subject with us – but I believe he thought I was turning into Escoffier, or wanting to, and he always loved mockingly to burst one's bubble.

One resents the cavil that makes idiosyncrasy out of individuality. I mean, why should Emily Dickinson *not* have sat in the dim hallway to listen to Mrs. Mabel Loomis Todd's music? Worn her hair out of fashion? Sewed her verses into fascicles? Why not converse athwart a door? I say let a person sing while hummingbirds fly out of his mouth as long as he insists on being himself, never bartering away the wonderful soul we are born with which so many people wantonly give away in the course of their lives.

I often saw Gorey prepare meals, delicious and quite sophisticated dinners, when, over the years living in his cousin's house, spoon in mid-air, consulting an old stand-by Shaker cookbook, he took it as his job to cook the dinner meal for everybody, which most of the time included local guests. He was an efficient fellow who needed elbow room for chopping shallots for chowder or for fracting a chicken or for deglazing a roast beef pan. He liked to prepare meals, taking over the kitchen in the house on Millway, often on Sundays, and once ingeniously cooked an all-blue meal. It was at one such dinner when the extended family got into a mildly heated exchange – certain cousins of his were fairly right-wing – when employing the *argumentum ad verecundium* he righteously exclaimed, in a self-deprecating way, of course, "Wait a minute – I'm famous!" (The fact of the matter is that he was internationally celebrated and had world-wide fans, in Germany and Japan especially, where he is much translated. He would not have been convinced if he were told that one day his death would have been front-page news in the illustrious *Times* of London.) Gorey pleaded with everyone for the longest time to avoid eating veal, so that no one was surprised after he died that he had willed his money and any proceeds from art-sales to animal charities, specifically to the Animal Rescue League; the Xerces Society for Environmental Protection; and Bat Conservation International. He was capably domestic, as one generally has to be who lives alone. I believe that he shared with the late Robert Benchley an incompetence with most mechanical things. I do know that he was not "handy," as they say. He would fussify and fret with certain objects, but in vain.

Quotidian jobs became events for him. There was a sort of innocence about him who did not seem to know how a lot of things worked. The first

Top photo: EG with cousins at dinner. ca. 1962.

Bottom photo: EG with Roy Morton, husband of cousin Elizabeth, mid 1960s.

letter that he ever wrote to me, back in the winter of 1972, ended after one page with, "I'm in a state of fidgets and futility. Besides I have to feed the washing machine." I believe that he sought preoccupations in arts and crafts and such menial work as collecting objects and sewing things to take him away from other preoccupations, more serious things, knocking about in his head. Don't be fooled. No one with that matchless – and mad – imagination was simply Betty Crocker making buttermilk biscuits. He did not show it, but I have the feeling, let me add by way of footnote, that underneath all those crazed moans and stage groans beat the heart of a real anarchist, a revolutionary, a man of passion who knew far more than he ever said about the heart of darkness.

On this matter of Edward Gorey and menial work, he needed to manipulate and was obsessive-compulsive about using his fingers. It goes without saying that he seemed to find comfort in tactile repetition. While watching television, he could often be found stitching a stuffed figure or sewing beanbag animals of all sorts. Doing jigsaw puzzles was also a popular pastime with him. It became a small passion. He collected puzzles, in fact, going in less for themes than for shapes, colors, designs, the more challenging the better. I believe the artistic mind in looking at shapes is challenged by the lexicon of ordeals they present, Picasso, Braque, Mondrian, and people like Charles Burchfield who before his realistic period fixated on spirals, curves, ovals, and jagged lines to which he attributed specific emotions. Gorey was intrigued by the intricacy of the more complicated puzzles, and on occasion went so far as to take photographs of difficult puzzles after they were finished. He preferred the heavy-duty sort, 1000-piece-plus puzzles with great herds of zebras or stacks of beer cans, M.C. Escher-jobs, I gather, those of the "Where's Waldo?" variety. I have heard mention that he actually completed something called the "Three Bears at Night," a famously all-brown puzzle, although I have never seen or come across it. I can still see him in my mind's-eye at a table, determinedly bent over, that tall quizzical bald head, pale, wispy white hair, working a puzzle like little Kai, blue with cold, in the great hall of ice in Hans Christian Andersen's *The Snow Queen*, playing an endless solitary game, trying to fit shards of ice together like pieces of a broken mirror.

He sewed in a deft manner, as I say, sitting on a sofa in front of his television set, his flurrying fingers becoming the "language of pins," in couturier-speak, as he worked like Balenciaga, who in the matter of at-hand dressmaking could supposedly rip a suit apart with his thumbs and then within the bat of an eyelash splendidly remake it relying solely on the picture in his mind's eye. (A surrealistic ballet of fingertips – yes, just those! – configures in his compelling book, *The Raging Tide: or, The Black Doll's Imbroglio*.) It was a joy to see how content Gorey could be at work, chatting away as he worked with swift, stabbing, dactylar movements like the rhythmic jabs of sewing-machine strokes, the beanbag held daintily by the tips of those attentive, probing fingers, his dainty little pinkie crooked like a teacup handle. I always somehow heard whenever I watched him sew that way the incantation from Cocteau's *The Infernal Machine:* "I speak, I work, I wind, I unwind, I calculate, I muse, I weave, I winnow, I knit, I plait." Whether it was delicately drawing with his pen – I remember the exactitude with which in my sitting room he drew a bat in my early copy of Bram Stroker's *Dracula* – or sewing a bean-bag elephant, I often thought of the line from Djuna Barnes's *Nightwood,* a book we both greatly admired, "When she touched anything, her hand seemed to take the place of an eye."

"Apart from nature, geometry's all there *is,"* proclaimed the youthful and ranting Auden to Christopher Isherwood – one finds hyperbole in the declarations and even hears and something echoes of Oscar Wilde – but it might iterate values and ideas of Gorey found in his mentor on shape. "Geometry belongs to man. Man's got to assert himself against nature, all the time... Of course, I've absolutely no use for color. Only form. The only really exciting things are volumes and *shapes*... Poetry's got to be made up of images and form. I hate sunsets and flowers. And I loathe the sea. The sea is formless."

Regarding shapes, I recall Gorey pulsating with delight over the silent film *The Single Standard* (1929), starring Greta Garbo, Nils Asther, and Johnny Mack Brown, when he would began listing all the shapes – points, lines, curves, planes – of Twenties furniture, clothes, hats, shoes, which he likened to variegations in the zones of leaves. I have seen it and find the young Garbo playing the languid Arden at her very peak of her most incandescent beauty, that perfect face, magnificent forehead, and gorgeous fluffy hair. She craves liberation and strives for freedom, equality, the chance to be all that she can be. When she drives off on a lark with the handsome chauffeur to the country and kneels down and looks at the midnight moon – magnificent! It is a daring film. "I don't believe in half-measures," she declares, "I want to live

He exposed himself Lewdly.

She ran out of the room Tearfully.

From *The Glorious Nosebleed.*

honestly" – meaning *as I wish, wildly, outside convention.* "I'm walking alone because I *want* to walk alone" she snaps at an old bounder who tries to pick her up on a rainy street. Gorey loved the geometry of objects. Garbo's sailor cap, her aviator cloche, the robes she wore – zebra-striped, one with rows of arrows, etc. – the sheared wool jacket, the diamond bedroom door with its speed lines, the tuxes, ballrooms. You see a lot of her body. Those gorgeous legs. The rueful lips. *The Single Standard* is a movie Gorey would naturally love, for, although it ends with Arden, after a dangerous liaison with another man, choosing to remain with her husband and child – it is thematically an anti-*Anna Karenina* – the avant-garde spirit she embodies has its parallel with Gorey's own uncompromising life, the kind that is greeted with the kind of shock that people always reserve for those who, as Wordsworth once said, create the taste by which they are to be appreciated. Arden, beleaguered by attentive men, watched the male society surrounding her with the same gimlet eye by which she defied it and was as dubious as Gorey about being taken in by it.

One was never quite sure about Gorey and anonymity, however. He used to walk around Manhattan, quite conspicuously, with a full beard in a huge below-knee fur coat, big scarf, and tennis shoes. He was not what you would call a "furvert." I believe that he wore fur because he actually *liked* animals – that it was a way of being near them, nutty as you may find that explanation to be. There is surely a rich treasure for anyone to mine who wants to plumb the endless seams of the mystery or history of ambiguity – the twin selves – between a person's grandiosity and shyness, between self-mythologizing and solitude. (In Japan, an estimated 1.2 million people are part of the phenomenon of *hikikomori* or "social withdrawal," a problem often blamed on Japan's education system and social pressure to succeed.) In any case, I believe that a person may sprout another or parallel and not necessarily harmful personality to counteract one that tries to predominate, a sort of Hegelian-like counterweight, as it were, to keep the ship upright. As I have mentioned, the distinctive license plate on Gorey's yellow VW identified him, unambiguously, as "Ogdred." (I suggest it is no more reasonable to ask why he did not drive a brutally black plain old American Plymouth with an undistinguished license-plate number than to ponder why a fellow of such a high aesthetic could spend endless hours recording on VHS cassettes vapid shows of *Barnaby Jones*.) He was listed quite openly in the Cape Cod telephone directory. If he happened mistakenly to open his door to a passionate fan who stopped by, he could be obliging. I think this spontaneous availability may have been nothing more than the simple exertion of free will by a person who insisted that, no matter what, he be able to come and go as an ordinary person. It seemed a very important need. At the same time, I would also say that he had almost no faith in man. Cynicism, which has infected some of the world's deepest thinkers, may be the one disease of which one can never be cured. It may be the primal scream of the collector, among which group Gorey must certainly be numbered.

If persons and places mean nothing, that leaves, what – well, *things*, doesn't it? Gorey collected everything. Sad irons. Signs. Dolls. Telephone pole insulators. Masks. Puppets. The statue of an elephant. Big and little seashells. Eggs. Cape Cod candles. Paintings. Odd ashtrays. CDs. He deeply loved chunks of architecture – rare examples of Victorian gingerbread, entablature, cornices, dentil molding, dormer pieces, and so forth. Another strange collectible that excited him was decorative finials, for lamps, swifts, curtain rods, roofs, pots, Torah finials, newel caps, general blacksmithiana, and cobbling tools, etc. He had a mummy's hand in a case! ("Peter Paul Rubens – read his letters – had a whole mummy in his possessions!" Gorey told me once.) His small house was filled to overflowing with all sorts of objects. He *used* them in instances for his art. Many of the objects in his rooms, tassels, masks, shells, etc. appeared in the drawings in his books. A 1963 feature story in the *New York Herald Tribune* reported that his apartment in the Murray Hill section contained at the time five large brown-and-white framed lithographs of Peruvian mummies, a large white crucifix without a face, and furry animal dolls. Everywhere in his rooms were stacks of LP's, videocassettes, trunks filled with varieties of utensils. "I buy those quite cheap at yard sales," he told interviewer Clifford Ross, who asked him what sort of utensils. Gorey, who through the course of his life had a sort of *horror vacui* thing going on, replied, "I don't know, anything from pliers to large wrought-iron things that hold those hinges on doors. And stuffed animals I've found occasionally at antique shows." He had a collection of skulls of all sorts and shapes, an array of old ginger jars in his kitchen, with its walls of antique gray tones, and no end of books, books by the thousands – books, books, books! ("Thank God for books as an alternative to conversation," Auden said. "The annual tonnage of publications is terrifying if I think about it, but I don't have to think about it. That is one of the wonderful things about the written word: it cannot speak until it is spoken to." Did Gorey own a real human skull? Yes. Did it take pride of place irreverently wearing a pair of specs? Take one guess. At one point years ago, I saw a whole roomful of balls! He loved blue glass, and one saw groupings of blue bottles and blue dishes everywhere. There were also cheese graters that he had collected, many of them in a row. That was the fire-spark, you see. Objects placed together become an "installation." It was the *cumulative* effect that pleased Gorey. Was collecting a "security obsession," poet Marianne Moore's favorite explanation for her own particular assembling or gathering proclivities when she was once asked why she always wore two watches, a Hamilton and an Eternamatic? I frankly think of such large collections as the neurotic's way of having – and taking care of – children.

He collected antique Japanese *okimono*, enchanting miniature sculptures crafted in metals such as bronze and silver, ivory, bone and ceramic, and had a small collection of sand-paintings. I know that he went through an elephant phase and collected all sorts of pachyderms at one time. He collected African art: masks, textiles, game-boards, the odd spear or two. He kept bags and bags of *fabrics* in his attic, I remember, Thai silks, Provençal prints, batiks, anything. To him more or less everything was art and his egalitarian tastes regarding what he loved to collect included a refrigerator covered with all sorts of magnets – magnets of clenched fists, porcelain magnets with recipes on them, magnets of hearts. (A big hole in the lower part of the temple of this fridge had been worn away, incidentally, by the corrosives of cat piss!) The array of cat-food dishes that always faced a pair of cast-iron dog andirons – Gorey throve on irony – might well have constituted part of a collection of them, for all I know. His collection of copies of Nancy Drew and The Rover Boys books kept some kind of flame alive; I remember his telling me several times how, having first read The Rover Boys at summer camp in 1934, he was hooked for life. He drew little distinction between human beings and characters out of books, and he would refer to Nixon or Von Moltke or Charles V in the same sentences and with equal force as the Green Hornet and Henry Aldrich and Dagwood Bumstead. He loved assemblages. He collected cast-iron hippos, rocks that looked like toads, bells, balls, bowls of many sizes. I was shown part of these collections by Ken Morton, to whom I have already alluded. One extraordinary grouping was a small coin collection, which Ken kept in a heavy folder. It held stone coins, metal coins, clay coins, a Mysia, Parion with laureate heads of Apollo; Celtic Durotriges – ancient British coins from the 1ˢᵗ century – several examples of Chinese "Ant Nose Money," copper coins from 600 B.C.; ancient orichalcum coins of the Roman republic. I saw a Philip of Macedon II coin from 359-336 B.C. E.; a Byzantine Lead Seal ca. A.D. 900-1000; and various and sundry coins of bare-head Drusus. He had for some reason or another also fixated exclusively on collecting as many coins as he could of one particular Roman emperor named Trebonianus Gallus, Roman Emperor from 251 to 253, who had been executed by his own troops and thrown in a latrine! He collected stuffed animals – "I collect Teddy Bears in a desultory sort of way," he told one interviewer – and he would often palpate a favorite stuffed toy lion during interviews. He once sewed a toy elephant from an old discarded Brooks Brothers shirt which had the tiniest stitches, revealing an expertise in fine sewing. Animals, I repeat, meant everything to him. He was a tender man. He cried all the way home when his cat, "Charlie," died, and seemed disoriented for weeks.

Calm and unpretentious, Gorey was exclusive but never a snob. He wore old shirts and jeans, drove a humble Volkswagen "Golf," and lived in a simple house in Yarmouthport, Massachusetts to which any and all eager Mr. Quiverfuls of Puddingdale with a single knock had access. I never saw the man wear a necktie or a suit in twenty-five years. There were no stories that way. A photograph of him dressed formally would be a keepsake. He for some reason liked cut-off jean shorts. He eventually jettisoned wearing raccoon fur coats later in life, feeling guilty wearing fur. (After his death, there were as many as fifteen full fur coats of his found to be in cold storage.) I recall him once ordering from a catalogue a sweatshirt that had the phrase "*Carpe Diem*" sloganized on it and he was slightly irked when he received it in the mail that the Latin phrase, for the obtuse, no doubt, was translated into English underneath. He could discuss *The Simpsons* or the worth of the old actor James Gleason with the same passion he had in discussing the feats of brave Roald Amundsen or the intrepid Reinhold Messner, the greatest climber of all time, and that he brought to an explanation of what Ludwig Wittgenstein meant by the "synopsis of trivialities." A wide reader is always a polymath. Any given conversation with Gorey could range from – as it once did and which I made note of – the geometry of cat's ears to G.W. Pabst's film technique, *Little Lulu*, Jacob Bronowski on the age of huts, low water levels on Cape Cod, who danced Giselle in 1911, and the invincible vulgarity of the preposterous Kathie Lee Gifford and the host of miniature

Top photo: EG in Cape Cod meadow, ca. 1968.

Bottom photo: EG with cousin Eleanor and her mother, 1960s.

faces she was constantly pulling. As I said, he bought a satellite dish for his roof to get hundreds of channels on his television set. "I'm a gadabout. I love having *The X-Files* on tape and stuff. *The Golden Girls* may have fallen off a bit, but they're still marvelous. I think TV movies tend to be better than regular movies these days, don't you? I mean, big screen costs have gone absolutely haywire and what do you get, a few twiddly innovations, a car chase or two, and that's it, folks." He laughed. "Who would have thought back in the Thirties that Son of Cinecolor would be the rage of the Seventies? And since then, *un maigre repas, un maigre repas,* dear Alex, who suddenly looks worried, or don't you think you agree?" (Wrong: I tended to agree with virtually everything he said.)

He was the only person I have ever known who actually liked television commercials – I seem to recall he was for a time even involved in actually taping some of them, or at least certain favorites – and was as much at home gabbing about their "art," the packaging and the plots, as with Mondrian, the French cinema of horror, or the novels of Henry Fielding. I know that for a long time he recorded tapes of *Buffy The Vampire Slayer* episodes, for which he had a passion. You could not like or admire Gorey if you had a horror of primness. Nor of excess. You had to reshuffle your ideas of priorities to understand him. It takes someone like Henry James to put into words Gorey's value system when he wrote it is "in the waste of time, of passion, of curiosity, of contact that true initiation resides," and so it follows that no scene, strange accent, no adventure – experienced or vicarious – is irrelevant.

Gorey, who came into his essential intellectual life just about the time Sartre and Camus were popular on a worldwide scale, found most everything about human nature absurd. Politics. Sports. Trends and fads. International news. Chat shows. Oh, he watched them or, better, was aware of them. But he was a born *isolato* and his singular fascinations – books, movies, music, television, antiques, art – involved solitary commitment and had virtually nothing to do with people in the sense of directly encountering them. I believe that he subscribed to the condition that Joseph Conrad described, "We live, as we dream – alone." I also noticed over the years, nevertheless, that when any major catastrophe took place, horrors like the loony Heaven's Gate Cult Suicides or the Yorkshire Ripper murders or the Jonestown Massacre in Guyana, he was somehow always the first to know about them and always had an apt comment. He was altruistic, as I have noted, but always a realist. He was also, to repeat, a political liberal, but like any perceptive person he was also savvy and never questioned the fact, say, that all politicians are without exception greedy self-serving morons and complete hypocrites ("Show-business people without the talent," he once said). He paid no dumb homage to anything. He had a singular grasp of the verities. Rapacity destroys what it is successful in acquiring. We mainly criticize in others the very vices we ourselves have. Man is a wolf to man. I do have to say that corrupt politicians exercised him like others never could. I once pointed out to him that even Thomas Jefferson, scandalously, did not fight in the Revolutionary War, and Gorey's response, charitable, was, "Didn't he spend all that time inventing water clocks?" I vividly recall when I first interviewed Gorey in the early Seventies and Watergate was in full swing how he paused at one point, flung a leg over a chair, exhaled, and declared, "Nixon" – the sigh came from his foot-sole – "works me up terribly." The pursuit of that subject, we both agreed, seemed profitless. And on the subject of religion?

"I don't believe in God in the Christian sense," he once declared. "I'm not terribly religious." God never says a word in the cosmology of Gorey; fathers, uncles, and severe guardians – his dexterous mouthpieces – do. Gorey's father, who worked for a Hearst newspaper and in public relations in Chicago, was a Roman Catholic, but the inexorability of that persuasion ended for Gorey in the second grade, he explained, when, packed off to church, he claimed he used to "throw up" – which became for him (gainsaying, this, the hagiographical commonplace which often links early illness to conversion) a memorable icon for the end of this Catholic period. Still, he had an aunt who was a nun. His mother was Episcopalian. His parents divorced when he was 11, then remarried sixteen years later. I found Gorey a secular person who gave off a sense of inner piety. He had a distinct latitudinarian outlook in the way he viewed pretty much everything. He was non-violent. "My philosophy? I'm a Taoist, if I'm anything," he told Mary Rourke of the *National Observer* in 1976. "They believe this is the way the world runs, and you might as well just go along with it. I stand by the idea that you can't prevent things. The Surrealist writers thought the most mysterious thing of all is just everyday life. I agree. Everyday life is very discomfiting. I guess I'm trying to convey that discomfiting texture in my books." It was an Heraclitean world to Edward Gorey. I could see it in the way he saw how movie stars wore it in their frayed garments of fame. As Samuel Johnson noted of the notion of ephemeral celebrities, "They mount, they shine, evaporate, and fall." It is the "all flesh is grass" idea. We are here but briefly. Fleeting ghosts. In the succinct words of H.D. in "Leda" from *Hymen*:

> *Though Sparta enter Athens,*
> *Thebes wreck Sparta,*
> *each change as water,*
> *salt, rising to wreak terror*
> *and fall back*

He read Thomas Merton, had certainly imbibed a lot of Nietzsche, showed himself more than well-acquainted with the Chinese translator Arthur Waley's *Three Ways of Thought in Ancient China*, and I have seen him with a copy of the extracts of Chung Tzu. Gorey had a Buddhist's gentleness and cosmic sense of acceptance. I believe his search for tranquil belief combined with a constant protest against the actualities of experience.

I gather that ultimately he found no reason to believe in anything religious except a human desire to avoid "deep-seated despair." He fobbed off our foibles on no one but ourselves and our own hapless thumbfumbling. There was a gnosticism at work, perhaps, his sense that in this enigmatic and inspissated universe we are alone, that the ultimate God is beyond good and evil and infinitely remote from creation. It was not icy-hearted nihilism. There is something puerile in Nihilism. Cobbled together out of scraps of determinism, vanity, and a kind of self-protective complacency, and sad existential burnout, it barely deserves the name of philosophical doctrine. Observing the universe, Gorey was more inclined to self-reproach, too diffident to be vain, too intelligent not to see the lambent contrast – or better perhaps, similarities – between the questions we do not ask and the answers we are afraid to hear. In the novel *Of Human Bondage* Philip Carey prayed God would cure him of his clubfoot and was disappointed it did not happen, and Maugham wrote, "The impotence of man to govern or restrain the emotions I call bondage, for a man who is under control is not his own master." I think Gorey subscribed to that idea. But would you like my opinion? It is my personal belief, obstreperous if you choose to say so, that *nobody* does not believe in God. As I am speaking for myself, I will clarify that I speak for nobody else. Gorey did often repeat to many, "I have always been a firm believer in a line from a Patrick White novel, 'Life is full of alternatives, but

Illustration from a Christmas card.

no choice.'" He'd wave a hand. "I think you have to rely on chance an awful lot. I don't really believe in free will." It is all presented to us, with variations. The power that makes the future consumes the present and renders the past a lonely sorrow. We read that "the saddest story of them all is what might have been." Nothing "might have been." What is, is, and what might have been never could have existed. We do not really choose to be attracted to someone. We pursue ourselves, following what we are. Nothing is as it seems. I agreed. I told him that Waley was actually a Jew from Tunbridge Wells – Arthur David Schloss – who changed his surname to his paternal grandmother's maiden name. Gorey seemed surprised but saw I was a reader, something of a seeker even, and we became friends.

O nce I told him I had had a dream where God was a human lord and instead of humans we were all cats on this earth, fearful, anxious, running about, snarling. Could this have been my concept of eternity, and was it ailurophilic or ailurophobic? Comically, Gorey asked if I had a prie-dieu in my house and turning to me then inquired with a lilt of irony but giving his words something of a sonic halo, "Do you kneel to pray, Alex, and, do tell me, is it an exercise that still goes on with suitable agony and certainty of address?"

My reply was to leave a copy of *Mr. Fortune's Maggot* on his doorstep the next day with an accompanying note-card directing his attention to a small passage on page 15: "God winnows the souls of men with the beauty of this world: the chaff is blown away, the true grain lies still and adoring."

I believe I can say he liked my books and even found a lot of my theories cogent and, one would like to think, even compelling. I remember that he agreed with me that there are four distinct sexes: men, women, gays, and female singers – a grouping all of their own as far as vain, tempestuous divas go, all those petty, hard-to-handle singers like Dinah Washington, Billie Holiday, Nina Simone, Maria Callas, and too many others still alive, fierce, endlessly demanding, and complicated intransigents to a one, who, floral beyond words, often spiteful, are given to the kind of legendary conniptions and impossible behavior we tend to associate with the jealous, dominating, but beautiful Queen Grimhilde in Walt Disney's *Snow White* who disguises herself as an old hag and uses a poisoned apple to "kill" Snow White, the actual *stepmother* of Snow White, remember – she had seduced and married a widowed king, who had a daughter called Snow White with his first wife, and then after the king died, the Queen ordered Snow White off to work in her castle, forcing her stepdaughter to abandon her title as Princess. I mention this because whenever I did air one of my theories (and there were and are many) Gorey always registered his smirking approval with a bout of exaggerated applause – slow steady hand-clapping – and the comically deflating, "Now shall we have a rum shrub?"

It was not *schadenfreude*. He was far from cruel. I have also tried to put paid to any idea that, while he could be melancholy, he was morbid, not in the way, certainly, that a person such as, say, Ralph Waldo Emerson was, a man who as a youngster was early initiated into the culture of death, always a Victorian preoccupation – Transcendentalism which fetishized grief had a strong necrophiliac tropism – for it is well-known that Emerson was strongly influenced by an aunt who wore her own shroud while alive and slept in a coffin-bed. (He once went so far as to dig up his son's body, after its decay, to contemplate it and, later, even exhumed his wife Lidian's body, out of morbid nostalgia.) It is remarkable while pondering the matter of Emerson to contemplate in his essay, "Thoreau," an encomium that constitutes an elegy of his neighbor, the great naturalist and eccentric, to see how many of Thoreau's personal characteristics seem so closely to parallel and/or resemble those of Edward Gorey:

> *He was bred to no profession; he never married; he lived alone; he never went to church; he never voted…He chose, wisely no doubt for himself, to be the bachelor of thought and Nature. He had no talent for wealth, and knew how to be poor without the least hint of squalor or inelegance…A fine house, dress, the manners and talk of highly cultivated people were all thrown away on him…He wanted a fallacy to expose, a blunder to pillory, I may say required a little sense of victory, a roll of the drum, to call his powers into full exercise. It cost him nothing to say No; indeed he found it much easier than to say Yes.*

Gorey, who was, needless to say, neither a rustic nor a revolutionary, did sporadically attend art school, was not poor, although he was by no means rich, and of course did campaign and vote for Adlai Stevenson in 1952, as I have mentioned, but in his uncompromising and strange individualism, his flat refusal to live by society's formulations, his inveterate

The natives, afterwards, took fright
When she was seen, off shore, at night.

From *The Tuning Fork.*

insistence on questioning everything, and his avoidance of living by and for orthodoxy's rules, was in many ways a good deal like the Sage of Walden.

I think Gorey was a total skeptic. He held out for *no* absolutes. I think he loved the subject of modal logic, of obligation, permission, and time. He preferred to see trees without their foliage, as Abraham Lincoln famously did who for that arguably morbid preference explained that "their anatomy could then be studied." Gorey's books are essentially Fortean in nature, with their dark, brooding landscapes, quirky characters, and mysteries often left unsolved. Books of his such as *The Tuning Fork*, *La Malle Saignante*, *The Just Dessert*, and *The Stupid Joke* are nothing less than epistemological fables. Serious existential questions in his work are always being asked, even if they are not answered. Was Ludwig Wittgenstein wrong when he stated, "It is a mistake to conceive of meaning as essentially tied to the nature of reality"? Gorey in his natural sanity and sublime oddity was surely right to be cynical. The Christian idea, to be in the world, not of it, is an idea not only sound but a policy required to maintain one's personal ethics, never mind one's own sanity. The world is all wrong. Upsidedown. Corrupt. Bought. Sold. Over a lifetime I have witnessed the preference of mediocrity over merit. Congress, a self-serving body composed mostly of half-wits, can still legally take bribes from "lobbyists," and venal politicians, both local and national, see to it that their own names, never artists or scientists or inventors, are memorialized on tunnels, airports, and buildings. Dunces preside over important national legislation, with every vote polemicized as Red and Blue states rarely consider the welfare of the nation as a whole. In an essentially Protestant country, there is presently not a single Protestant on the U.S. Supreme Court. Television programs are geared to the empty skulls of 12-year-olds, and it is a commonplace to hear national broadcasters making grammatical errors. Merit nowadays is measured by success and success solely by money. Appallingly bad movie actors are paid lordly fortunes for a single film. "Tiger" Woods is rated the #1 golfer in the world solely by dint of wealth, accrued by endorsements and deals. Baseball players batting not even their weight are earning millions of dollars a season, while hundreds of others, taking steroids – Bud Selig, the baseball commissioner, has idly stood by now while *cheating* has been going on in baseball for decades – are forgiven, as long as a player apologizes, and only after he is caught. Open prejudice against all Moslems is cheerfully accepted in the United States now, openly allowed on American radio and television, and racist terms like "Islamic fanatics" and

"Moslem fanatics" is in constant use daily, but if you should say just once "Jewish fanatics" or "Israeli fanatics" you would be instantly fired and roundly condemned and possibly arrested for a hate crime. Animals, no longer grass-fed, are fat-stuffed with hormones, making their intestinal tracts more acidic, which favors the growth of pathogenic E. coli bacteria, which in turn is killing people. Breakfasts cereals are sugar. Our oceans are badly overfished, with massive "dead zones" found within them, oxygenless plumes as long as hundreds of miles, filled with debris and fertilizer run-off so polluted that virtually nothing there is alive. Bee populations are dying out from diseases, parasites, and pesticides, there is an alarming decline of songbirds in North America, and the oil-spill in the Gulf of Mexico will breed ruin for decades to come. Art galleries take as much as 50% from artists, literary agents are pimps, most cops are badly overweight, many priests are child-molesters, and Christmas as a holiday has been expunged by secularism. There is now a huge hotel in Monument Valley.

An epiphany of true despair came to me one night when, looking into Richard Schickel's biography, *Elia Kazan*, I wondered exactly what reality amounts to, never mind honesty, when I read: "One night, [screenwriter Budd] Schulberg remembered, 'I was talking about my old man and [Will Rogers, Jr.] was talking about his father, and he said, 'My father was so full of shit, because he pretends he's just one of the people, just one of the guys…but in our house the only people that ever came as guests were the richest people in town, the bankers and the power-brokers of L.A. And those were his friends and that's where his heart is and he was really a goddamned reactionary.'" *Will Rogers!?* I asked myself, if this is the case with a tree that is (supposedly) green, what of those that are dry?

I know Gorey believed that change is continual, permanence does not exist in the universe, and that men in a state of nature do not easily know good or evil, having only their independence to probe. Gorey and I discussed faith, often. I understand that he thought I regarded him as a Laodicean, neutral in the matter of faith. I do, however, recall one Saturday morning many summers ago driving through Orleans with him and as we passed the stately white United Methodist Church hearing over the carillon the bells playing, "A Mighty Fortress is Our God." He primly folded his hands across his knee, enigmatically looked out the passenger window, and said, "There may be salvation yet."

The cognitive quality of Edward Gorey's books, that strange dark art opulently, often contagiously assembled out of his searching mind – the seven-zephyred suavity of his impeccable drawings and exact texts – rise in the matter of the macabre so much higher than all of those bulbous not-quites – hideously lacking all conviction *while* full of passionate intensity – like Stephen King and Dean Koontz, Robin Cook and James Patterson, and their crapulous, hand-cranked, artless, throw-it-up-in-the-air-to-see-what-comes-down doorbuster books stuffed with high-school hoodoo and toy horror. He did not crank out shlock with big red hands, nothing like it. He was a diamond engraver. It was his gift to probe the heart of where people remember truths. As Van Veen writes in Nabokov's novel, *Ada, or Ardor,* reality is always "a form of memory, even at the moment of its perception."

Several publishers, among which can be numbered Little, Brown; Dodd Mead; Bobbs-Merrill; Simon & Schuster; even Doubleday took up Gorey and then abandoned him, but undaunted, he kept working and in the Sixties came up with some splendid books like *The Bug Book* (1959); *The Willowdale Handcar* (1962); *The Vinegar Works* (1963), a boxed trilogy; *The Wuggly Ump* (1963); *[The Nursery Frieze]* (1964) – Gorey once told me that this little book whose title is always bracketed, was his favorite – that and *The Epiplectic Bicycle* (1969). Besides the Fantod Press, he undertook another venture: Between 1959 and 1962, he created the Looking Glass Library imprint with the help of Jason Epstein and Celia Carroll. In 1961 he published *The Curious Sofa,* subtitled "A Pornographic Work," "an exercise in cheerful silliness," as one critic has described it, a story in which nothing is explicit ("Still later, Gerald did a terrible thing to Elsie with a saucepan"). Notice in that book that it is only by suggestion and our own lewd or suggestible projected thoughts that we can find anything perverse in the book, which is of course what the author banks on. There is not a lewd word in the book, nothing coarse, no "Eskimo" talk, as Frank B. Galbreth Jr. so endearingly puts it in *Cheaper by the Dozen.* Gorey wrote the story and did the drawings over a weekend. "People always used to approach me to illustrate pornographic novels after that," says Gorey, "and I would reply, 'Have you chanced to look at that book?' The men are totally indistinguishable from the women. Everybody is seen from behind. That's the whole point. I think more than anything else it's really about a girl who's got an obsession for grapes." Some of my favorite Gorey illustrations are in books that over the years he has illustrated for other writers, like Edmund Wilson's *The Rats of Rutland Grange* (1974); H. G. Wells's *The War of the Worlds;* Samuel

From Jane Trahey and Daren Pierce's rare
Son of the Martini Cookbook.

Beckett's *All Strange Away* (1976); Jane Trahey and Daren Pierce's rare *Son of the Martini Cookbook* (n.d.), a part fold-out oversize published by Clovis Press – I bought my copy (my favorite of all his books) for $20 in a bookstore on West 18th St. in Manhattan in 1975 – and Edward Lear's marvelous fables *The Jumblies* (1968) and *The Dong With the Luminous Nose* (1969).

Strange tiny books of his have appeared under various pseudonyms. For example, *The Floating Elephant* (1993) by Dogear Wryde is a wordless flip-book – a series of pictures that vary gradually from one page to the next, simulating motion – that shows a small elephant being launched into space. Reverse the book to find *The Dancing Rock* (1993) by Ogdred Weary – Gorey always saw to it that he inscribed each such book with the stated alias – another wordless ballet, by way of the flip-book, showing a single boulder in motion. Gorey's midget kineographs are all invariably satirical, lampooning one thing or another. There is *The Pointless Book: or, Nature & Art* (1993) by Garrod Weedy, "In Two Volumes Bound Together," (size 2" x 1 ½), another micro-book, on every page a meaningless squiggle, each one portentously framed, to mock conceptual art and the fakers who make it. *Figbash Acrobate* (1994) by Aewyrd Goré, when you flip the pages, records the acrobatics of his long-armed, anteater-nosed, signature creature, Figbash.

His experiments with books – pop-up books, wordless books, books literally matchbox-sized, elongated books, books of cards, books entirely populated by inanimate objects, etc. – all serve his vision. Almost all his early books were done in black-and-white. "Partly the reason I did not work in color for a long time was that, since I was working at Doubleday, I knew only too well that if nobody knew who you were or anything, they were not going to publish books in color." Much of his later work was done in color, notably *The Broken Spoke* (1979); his great pop-up book, *The Dwindling Party* (1982); and *The Haunted Tea-Cosy* (1997) in which parsimonious bachelor Edmund Gravel, the Recluse of Lower Spigot – initials noted – is visited by Christmas ghosts, one muttering, "I am the Spectre of Christmas That Never Was and I have come to show you Affecting Scenes."

He was a scrutineer, his work going from concise energetic joy to irreverent disgust to a mockery of seemliness to a send-up of art to innocent bluffing to shuddering wistfulness to fangless fun. With a magical flourish he went from productions of gnomic verse to brilliant limericks to beast fables to mystery kits to French symbolist plays to the pavannes of ballerinas. He fashioned hornbooks, abecedaria, pop-up stories with paper-engineering, flip-books, card decks, and tales narrated with post-cards. There is actually no one I can think of who draws quite like Edward Gorey. Consensus can find candidates. There are certainly those one may point to with kinship for the same tidy exactitude and incontrovertible searing wit, such as Hilaire Belloc or the brilliant Australian cartoonist Patrick Oliphant or the late Roland Topor, who however basically dabbled. Virgil Partch had the same off-beat genius. So did Ronald Searle. R. Crumb is inimitable. I have loved the work of George Cruikshank, Jimmy Hatlo, Al Capp, Rube Goldberg, Dr. Seuss, and grew up gleefully racing to turn the pages to see the colorful creations of Elmer Rache and Lang Campbell who did the Uncle Wiggily cartoons – Alice Wibblewobble, Dottie and Munchie Trot. Nurse Jane Fuzzy Wuzzy, and The Magoosielum ("The only thing that will drive away a Magoosielum is pineapple cheese, and Baby Bunty has none of that."). N.C. Wyeth, Edmund Dulac, and Arthur Rackham were matchless geniuses, all in a class of their own. But I honestly believe that for sheer uninfringeable originality and style no one can match any of those panels of refined black line, pages like theater sets, or the unique off-kilter panache of Edward Gorey. Notice the layouts. His works are marvels of finish. Balance is master.

I know several people, bright and witty people, who cannot fathom many of Gorey's stories, although they may have been intrigued with their meticulousness. One friend of mine feels that he shows his true sympathies in the little *poems*, reveals himself best there. Others think that much of his work (not his best) is pastiche.

I have always thought that, for the most part, he was not only as original as Aubrey Beardsley but in his sheer black and white world something of a co-religionist. The boldness and daring anti-philistinism they share is only the beginning. There is in the precision of the fine line, the infinite care, and the matchless style of both artists – the daring – nothing less than graphic genius. Both men if not basically reclusive were quiet and unassuming, both were of a fey disposition, both were fascinated with amateur theater, both did some acting, loved the theater, and illustrated theatrical posters, and of course both had a pronounced appetite for the impish, the risqué, and the scandalous. The decorative aspect in the work of both was nothing less than fetishistic. A curious note is that neither chose to paint, although Beardsley did leave us two surrealistic oils of masked women wearing black! It would be difficult to find anywhere two greater masters of the fastidious line, the almost erotically charged attention to imposing detail. Just to take one significant example, consider the fully achieved drawing of Beardsley's aristocratic but smug *The Abbé*, published in *The Savoy*, No. 1 with its amazingly detailed fretwork of butterflies, flowers, plumes and compare it with, say, Gorey's splendid alphabet book, *The Glorious Nosebleed*, a collection of 26 couplets. In the letter "J " entry, "She toyed with her beads Jadedly," a bearded man wearing an elaborate quilted fur – something like 200 separate quilted segments are revealed! – is presenting a roasted bear's head on a platter to a jaded women looking away bored and toying with a string of pearls around her neck. A rug of mad designs is spread on the floor. Fat tassels depend from a singular array of thick drapes embroidered with mad squiggles. Such work! Look at the density of illustration in Gorey's *The Blue Aspic, The Other Statue,* and *Scenes de Ballet,* as fine as anything as Beardsley has done. In many of Gorey books can also be found Beardsleyan decadence and raffishness, especially works like *The Insect God, The Willowdale Handcar, The Doubtful Guest, The Gilded Bat, The Haunted Tea-Cosy, The Prune People, The Eclectic Abecedarium, The Broken Spoke, The Chinese Obelisk, The West Wing, Le Mélange Funeste,* and *L'Heure Bleue.*

I find very Goreyesque D.H. Lawrence's comment in his 1929 book of poems, *Pansies* (punning on Pascal's *Penseés),* when he points out that "flowers, to my thinking, are not merely pretty-pretty. They have in their fragrance an earthiness of the humus and the corruptive earth from which they spring. And pansies, in their streaked faces, have a look of many things besides hearts-ease." A creature can be found lurking in every Gorey garden, a doubtful guest in every room, a bloody axe or a hatchet among tools in the back shed. He saw what Harold Pinter called "the weasel under the cocktail cabinet."

The macabre intrigued Bearsdsley. His illustrations for Oscar Wilde's *Salome,* drawn to the playwright's original text, while witty, are also intentionally provocative and always daring. The mannerist mode that fit the Beardsley of the 1890s Gorey picked up without dropping a stitch. In the baroque furniture of their minds we see the same passion for the brilliant use of space to best set off illustrations that may show in one instance nothing but a single flower and then in another an explosive, cross-hatched, over-the-top caricature that positively fills – and occludes – the page! An hilarious spoof called *Oscar Wilde's Salome,* a Gorey adaptation "preceded by a puppet

THEATER ON THE BAY presents,
preceded by a puppet production of
SIX WHO PASS WHILE THE LENTILS BOIL
by Stewart Walker,

OSCAR WILDE'S
SALOME

Designed
and directed by
EDWARD GOREY

Music by
STRAVINSKY
and STRAUSS

Friday & Saturday at 8PM, Sunday at 5:30 PM
February 3-5, 10-12, 17-19, 1995

Trading Post Corners, Monument Beach (Bourne) MA

Tickets $10   Reservations (508) 759-0977

EG's *Salome* was first performed in 1995.

production of "Six Who Pass While Lentils Boil," was in fact performed in February 1995 by Theater on the Bay Productions at Trading Post Corners in Bourne, Massachusetts. A ticket cost $10. A memorable Salome (male) the night I saw it was running about the stage spouting Gorey poetry and wearing a head-scarf à la Natasha Rambova! Gorey's *Les Passementeries Horribles* which features very ominous braids and silk embroideries looming over people and animals, peeking through windows at the unaware – he shared with Beardsley an almost fanatical fixation with tassels and wallpaper, urns and topiary, dress fashion and swollen flowers – has its vivid parallels in such work as Beardsley's precise drawings for *Volpone* and his illustrations to Poe's *The Murders in the Rue Morgue* along with his well-known self-portrait as a monstrous invalid, an infant voyeur peering out from a voluminous bed topped with breasts and a huge canopy covered with tassels. Rococo plays into baroque. Talk about "pied beauty."

Irony with both of them was a corrective. Punning posters, they both loved. They loved to shock, to unsettle, to disturb, and not caring – on occasion *flagrantly* not caring – went a long way to boost their morale. Both were anti-bourgeois in the extreme, and to both artists, even if separated by a hundred years, the likeable but artistically sterile conviction that social fervor, good moral intentions, hard work, and literal-minded honesty would do as substitutes of talent put them both off. They certainly both had great fun with subject of sex. I have to say that my favorite Beardsley drawing is of the bisexual, transvestite heroine of Théophile Gautier's *Mademoiselle de Maupin*. Those *Salome* drawings, connecting him to the notorious Wilde, cost him jobs and badly hurt his reputation. "Their sexual tastes were compatible though not identical," notes Brigid Brophy in *Beardsley and His World*. "Beardsley's, which may well have been expressed chiefly in fantasy, were probably for the most part heterosexual, perhaps tinged with transvestitism. Performing his duty to shock [his publisher John] Lane, he wrote to him: 'I'm going to Jimmie's (the St. James's Restaurant) on Thursday night dressed up as a tart and mean to have a regular spree.'" A brooding if comic unwholesomeness infects many of Gorey's books, as well. Men incongruously appear in dresses, we see women with mustaches. A hedge looms to prevent us from taking in an indelicate scene. A naked leg appears from behind a curtain. Something untoward is suggested in books like *The Deranged Cousins, The Iron Tonic, The Loathsome Couple*, and *The Disrespectful Summons*. I have mentioned his great Dadaist book, *The Curious Sofa: A Pornographic Work* by Ogdred Weary.

A piquant little fable, it recounts the tale of a young girl Alice who, seduced into a world of bisexual orgies, is taken into a room with a "curious sofa" where something unclear and unspeakable happens. Every image has a caption, and almost every caption suggests some kind of sexual activity without going into lurid detail. It is literally "suggestive," something Gorey has always worked. Nothing sexual takes place. One of the joys of reading it is to keep track of all the euphemisms that he deploys for "well-hung." Beardsley also loved phalloi. Some of his best known work shows handsome naked men ostentatiously *en l'air* and he did not shrink from stark even if mannered pornography.

Beardsley also wrote *Under the Hill,* an unfinished erotic tale loosely based on the legend of *Tannhäuser.* It was published in *The Savoy.* He alternated calling the book *The Story of Venus and Tannhäuser* and kept changing the hero's name from the Abbé Aubrey to the Chevalier Tannhäuser to the Abbé Fanfreluche. He never finished the book or ever really settled which of its versions was definitive because it was his personal erotic fantasy and to finish it would have been to relinquish life, according to Brigid Brophy. Renowned for its dark and perverse images and the grotesque erotic themes which he loved to explore, this fantasy novel is an account of the manner of state held by Madam Venus, Goddess and Meretrix, under the famous Horselberg, and containing the adventures of Tannhäuser in that Palace, his repentance, his journeying to Rome and return to the Loving Mountain. At one indelicate point Venus even masturbates a unicorn! Over the course of his brief life he was thought to be a "diabolical reveler in vices," wrongly, thought George Bernard Shaw whose phrase it was. Rumors followed Beardsley to his grave. Speculation about his sexuality even extended to the calumny that he had an incestuous relationship with his older sister, Mabel, a sometime actress and friend of W.B. Yeats, whom they said may have become pregnant by her brother and miscarried. While Beardsley was a wildly imaginative and at times intemperate fellow who frankly did relish doing phallic drawings and such, he was recognized by many as an "innocent" who simply came under the influence of the French Symbolists, the Poster Movement of the 1890s, and the work of many later-period Art Nouveau artists like Frank Pape and Harry Clarke. On his deathbed in Mentone in 1898 a chastened Beardsley who had become a Roman Catholic wrote to his friend, Leonard Smithers, a solicitor from Sheffield who had set up as a bookseller in London, surely one of the most touching and contrite letters ever penned:

Jesus is our Lord and Judge

Dear Friend,
I implore you to destroy all copies of Lysistrata and bad drawings.
Show this to Pollitt and conjure him to do the same. By all that is holy
all obscene drawings.

Aubrey Beardsley
In my death agony.

It is Brigid Brophy's idea that Beardsley's "polymorphous perversity" was connected to his smothering mother, Ellen Agnus [sic] Pitt Beardlsey. "The drawings owe their erotic force to the fact that, thanks to her continuing in the central place in his mental world, he was able to keep intact – and clearly not to be able to throw off – "the fierce son-to-mother eroticism of childhood."

Gorey never married. "I have never been emotionally involved with anyone," he told me in 1973 – I wonder if I ever believed that – pointing out how for more than ten years he could just about manage to shuttle fretfully in his automobile between his apartment in the Murray Hill section of New York City on Madison Avenue at 38th Street and quiet, occasionally bleak small village of Barnstable on Cape Cod. That is, until after thirty years living in New York City and finally deciding to live year-round on the Cape – based on the fact of Peter Martins having replaced George Balanchine, the ailing balletmaster of the New York City Ballet whom Gorey reverenced to the point of obsession, whom he almost automatically praised in virtually every interview, but who left the company in 1983 – he bought his own house in 1988 in Yarmouthport, the one that was once identifiable by all the long thatchy grass out front that threatened to consume the porch. The dark, six or seven-room house on No. 8 Strawberry Lane, resembling the houses in his books, is a strange, wooden, sort of ancestral-looking thing with cold angles and a chimney in the center. A gray satellite TV dish sat on the small roof. Various figures and figurines on the windowsills – notably a cheap ceramic bust of Dickens – faced looking out toward the street, and on the walls inside could be seen several of his own posters on the wall. For a while on the porch there once sat an ominous-looking welder's mask, chosen for its futuroidally scary presence! He liked his own work – tea he often served in "Edward Gorey" cups – merely hated discussing it. The house stands just up the street from a local book shop, where as a young bibliophile Gorey with time on his hands used to sort books for the fat oafish owner. It is now a museum called the Gorey House, visited by eight thousand visitors in 2009, where a fat 27-pound white cat named Ombledroom sits by the door and inspects all visitors. (Remember the couplet from *The Utter Zoo*, "The O is vast and white/ And therefore visible by night"?) I try to stay away from the Gorey House for no other reason than I find it unsettling to find the rooms mausoleumized to a degree and to find a friend raised after death to a Very Exalted Personage. I went there only one time. Tours are provided, and events are held in Gorey's name. Here you can see, among other things, Gorey's earliest known drawing, "The Sausage Train," along with the first book he ever self-published in 1937 at the age of 12. The Strawberry Lane house became a real home for him, at last, something of his own in the way of a house that Gorey had long needed. Every object in it was hand-picked and each represents his haphazard genius from the glass knobs and accumulator jars to the blue bottles and rare ashtrays to the biomorphic stones and lovely paintings to the delicate celadon bowls and plates of soup-green, mustard, and apricot-rose majolica. He was in many ways a faddist with unlimited energy.

The odd, the out-of-the-way, the rare, the oblique, held an undying charm for him. He was a *pasticheur par excellence,* and the contents of the place, taken altogether, recreate in a sense all the many turns of his eclectic mind and its many fascinations, subconsciously arranged (I suspect) more to reflect character than to create loveliness. That New York/Cape Cod trek that he so often had to make had become fitful. He always traveled with the cats he had at the time, namely Agrippina, Fujisubo, Kanzuke, Kokiden, and Murasake, most of them having been named from Lady Murasaki Shikibu's *The Tale of Genji*, the world's first novel and one of Gorey's favorite books. "What I don't like about cats is you can't organize them!" complains a character in Robert Coover's novel, *Whatever Happened to Gloomy Gus of the Chicago Bears?,* and it must have been delightful negotiating the Cross Bronx Expressway at rush hour, which is all the time, with a pile of filled cat cages in summer in a Volkswagen! He actually dedicated the drawings he did for Edward Lear's *The Dong With The Luminous Nose* (1969) to three of his cats, and for his own illustrations of cats – antic, bejerseyed, grinning – he was of course famous; they appear everywhere, in much of his work, tumbling over all those Gorey mugs, stamps, posters, postcards, and jackflipping most notably over the covers of *Amphigorey* (1972), *Amphigorey Two* (1975), *Amphigorey Also* (1993), and then *Amphigorey Again* (2006), those popular collections or anthologies that compile some certain books of his otherwise difficult to find.

The many cats who possessively roamed his house – "Down, dippy!" he would often squawk to one who was going somewhere he should not or "Lilly Daché in furs here is craving attention!" (he might turn here and peremptorily interject, "Do you know that Daché quote, 'When a girl ceases to blush, she has lost the most powerful charm of her beauty'?") or "Good Morning, Marmaduke!" to another who might have caught the movie reference – were fat, fussy, and damned important to him. "My anthropomorphic cats are really quite different from regular cats," he would pronounce. But all were

He went off contentedly licking his chops,

From *Story for Sara.*

colorful and quite predominated in taking his attention. I remember once giving an outdoor party in the Eighties to which Gorey was invited. Many of my guests, knowing he would be there, came expressly to meet him. After he arrived, pulling up in his yellow Volkswagen bug, he walked into the yard – he wore his usual summer gear, cut off jean-shorts, a plain shirt, white sneakers, maybe a bracelet or two, and a thousand or so lion rings on his fingers – made a bee-line straight for my handsome black cat, Rat, picked him up, nuzzled him warmly for about ten minutes after taking a short lateral walk, at some remove, and only then did he return to meet, quite off-hand and soberly, all the other bewilderedly quiet and surprised onlookers. I know that he liked Shar-Pei dogs with their distinctive features of deep wrinkles and blue-black tongues, and at one point he even wanted to buy a Jack Russell terrier – but then felt in the end that it would never find peaceful co-existence with his menagerie of cats.

I believe that it is something of a truism that literary folk commonly tend to associate with cats. The French literary critic Charles Augustine Sainte-Beuve always had his tea and a brioche at noon in the company of his cats, la Jolie, la Vielle, la Maigrotte, and his favorite Mignonne, and it was his habit freely to allow them to climb upon his table and walk among his papers. A chubby, short, red-haired then balding eccentric who never married (he suffered from hypospadias which rendered him incapable of normal coition) – he was "a clever man with the temper of a turkey," according to Barbey d'Aurevilly – Sainte-Beuve wrote wearing what the French call a *madras* or bandanna around his bald head and always shaved without a looking-glass he was so ugly. Carl Van Vechten, the gay novelist and erotic photographer of the 1920s and 30s who wrote *The Tiger in the House: A Cultural History of the Cat*, the lighthearted compendium of feline lore he published in 1920 and complemented in 1921 with *Lords of the Housetops: Thirteen Cat Tales*, his selection of feline fiction, exalted the cat, as his biographer Clive Fisher has pointed out, for, among other reasons, "only the cat among other domestic animals can inhabit cities without longing atavistically for the primal savannah, its ancient instincts for territorialism and predation satisfied in verminous alleys and serried metropolitan gardens." Ironically, Van Vechten so loved cats that after the age of 40 he could no longer keep them, as he could no longer bear psychologically to part with them. Animals, specifically cats, were for Gorey what they were to the naturalist Henry Beston, author of the classic *The Outermost House*

(1928), a book that chronicles a season spent living on the dunes of Cape Cod. He wrote,

> *For the animal shall not be measured by man. In a world older and more complete than ours they move finished and complete, gifted with extensions of the senses we have lost or never attained, living by voices we shall never hear. They are not brethren, they are not underlings; they are other nations, caught with ourselves in the net of life and time, fellow prisoners of the splendor and travail of the earth.*

I attended a party at my brother Paul's house in 1983, just after Lady Diana's wedding, when Gorey's highly amusing if satirical comments on the overlushness of the Princess's wedding gown (delicious acres of crushed ivory silk-tafetta and lace embroidered with mother-of-pearl sequence of pearls), something she herself very soon thereafter came to agree with, at first scandalized Tina Brown and Harold Evans who were also guests, having just more or less arrived at the time to take their respective positions with *Vanity Fair* and *New York Times* but who clearly had never quite met anybody like Edward Gorey with his wistful, somewhat dramatic manner, filled with hyperbole and curmudgeonly wit. My understanding was that they did not initially like him. They had never seen such a person. To their credit, they caught on quickly to the slant of his humor and soon everything went swimmingly. I can still see him in my mind's-eye walking to his car in the rain under a big cherry-handled cotton umbrella.

What can one ultimately say in defense of a person who with studied conviction quite unequivocally much preferred the company of cats over human company? Edward Gorey, "master of horrid inconsequentiality," as J. Hillis Miller once referred to him, was both intrigued by and greatly respected the bedeviling enigma of cats, their arch and independent refusals to comply or to respond to human stupidity, and that easily assumed sense of serenity that flows through them. "God knows that day-to-day reality is drab to the point of lunacy," said Gorey in reference to the obliqueness, the understatement, of his work and particularly to the mystery of all it portrays. "And that means that you have to leave an awful lot out. I have a fairly eccentric talent, but I do frankly try to tone it down rather than heighten it. Most people, I think, tend to take the opposite approach.... Classical Japanese literature concerns very much what is left out. The Chinese, the

Japanese. I have always felt that they were much better [than we in the West] at describing everyday reality. That's why cats are so wonderful. They can't talk. They have these mysterious lives going on that are only half-connected to you." It is a commonplace that those who have trouble with people seek the company of animals.

There is a long-held, ancestral Yankee term used by New Englanders, particularly people from Maine, getting ready for winter – it is called "housing-up." Women of the farms put in order select rooms to be unheated, so sealed off, stripping beds, folding away blankets not to be reused until Spring comes round. It is a preparation for the siege, a "fortress" established against the wind, cold, dark. In a sense, Gorey in the fastness of his house and I believe in his mind was metaphorically sealed off, not weirdly shuttered, unavailable, or secretively provisioned like the almost Carthusian-like Emily Dickinson, but in a sort of life-long retreat from the impositions of the world he did not want to abide, he withdrew.

As to Gorey's legendary detachment, it was always hard to tell what was what. I myself never saw him with a man. He did tell Richard Dyer in his 1984 interview that indeed there had been "emotional entanglements" in his life, but he added, "I don't wish to get into them." He went on to explain, "I'm always interested to hear about it when somebody I know gets involved in some totally bizarre relationship, but I know perfectly well I wouldn't want to do it. It is hard enough to sit down to work everyday, God knows, even if you are not emotionally involved. Whole stretches of your life go kerplunk when that happens. Sometimes I ask myself why I never ended up with somebody for the rest of my life, and then I realize that obviously I didn't want to, or I would have. I read books about crazed mass murderers, and say to myself, 'There but for the grace of God…' Well, not really. All I'd like to do is bop some people over the head. In one way I've never related to people or understood why they behave the way they do. Understand me; I think life is the pits, but I've been very fortunate. I don't have any responsibilities to anybody except myself, and I have done pretty much what I wanted to do. Fortunately I have never been into drink, drugs, and depravity. I've worked reasonably hard, though not as hard as I should have. I'd love to believe in the possibility of millions and millions of alternative universes…" Celibacy, according to St. Augustine, is the most blessed state. The world, he said, would be improved if all reproduction would cease. Gorey would have so acceded.

Then this on marriage: "Every (conjugal) couple forms a unit from which a single person is excluded," wrote Roland Barthes in 1977, briefly staying with his brother, Michel, and his wife, Rachel, in Urt, near Bayonne, after his mother died, an extremely painful time for him. Barthes's remark addresses the literal sense of a couple excluding a single person, but it also points to the idea that when a couple exists or comes into being something on the nature of the single people entering into that coupledom is also lost. I believe that is mainly what Gorey feared in any union he might have considered or maybe even sought for a time.

"I don't even know" was his answer to a question once put to him by a rude *Boston Globe* reporter when she baldly asked him, "Are you a homosexual?" – surely a perfect answer, *the* perfect answer, to an intrusive question. The oversimplifying and importunate question was asked at another time by a reporter hoping for a scoop for *Boston Magazine*, a parochial, gossip-filled city magazine that in trying to sell tickets to the city somehow never gets a story right, and Gorey answered her by saying, "Well, I'm neither one thing nor the other particularly. I am fortunate in that I am apparently reasonably undersexed or something…I've never said that I was gay, and I've never said that I wasn't… what I'm trying to say is that I am a person before I am anything else." Whenever I read that, and I have to say that I have heard variants of it over the years, I never fail to call to mind the stark title of Kierkegaard's *Either/Or* (Volumes I and II) for which Gorey famously did the well-known striking black-and-white cover and typography of the Doubleday Anchor original in 1959, a paperback edition I virtually grew up with.) On another occasion he rather blandly philosophized, "I realize that homosexuality is a serious problem for anyone who is [a homosexual] – but then, of course," he added, "heterosexuality is a serious problem for anyone who is [that], too. And being a man is a serious problem and being a woman is, too. Lots of things are problems." Edward Gorey agreed in another one of his interviews that the "sexlessness" of his books, whatever that meant, was a product of his own asexuality. One does however recall from *The Listing Attic* this memorable – and perhaps apposite? – limerick:

> *Said a girl who upon her divan*
> *Was attacked by a virile young man,*
> *"Such excess of passion*
> *Is quite out of fashion"*
> *And she fractured his wrist with her fan.*

"I tried it once and thought it was overrated. I mean, what's the big deal?" he said, according to one article I read. A friend of his from San Diego wrote to me correcting this. "'I tried it once and I was quite disappointed' is what he actually said." I cannot say that Gorey's attitude matched that of Somerset Maugham who once famously said that as a young man he had thought that he was "three quarters normal and that only a quarter of me was queer – whereas really it was the other way around." He was also older by more than a quarter century than the actor Nathan Lane, also Irish Catholic, who when he told his mother he was gay, she dolefully replied, "I'd rather you were dead," to which he replied, "I knew you'd understand." Lane, who came out publicly after the death of young Matthew Shepard, once jokingly explained, "I was born in 1956. I'm one of those old-fashioned homosexuals, not one of the newfangled ones who are born joining [pride] parades." Suffice it to say, Gorey saw no reason to pretend, but he also saw no reason to proclaim either. Whatever anyone chooses to refer to one – a bent, a gay, an invert, a chap Irish by birth but Greek by injection, etc. – I never saw him with a foop, a joy-boy, a shirtlifter, a poof, a puff, or a tootle-merchant, no one, neither an older man – no "dad" or an "afghan"– nor even a younger boy, a cupcake, a capon, or a Ganymede. I never saw him with a copy of John Horne Burns's *The Gallery* or *Funny Boy* by Shyam Selvadurai or *La Bâtarde* by Violette Leduc or *Queens* by Pickles or Aleister Crowley's *White Stains* or *René's Flesh* by Virgilio Piñera or John Preston's *Franny, the Queen of Provincetown*.

Did Gorey perhaps stand with the speaker in Shakespeare's "Sonnet 129" in which passion in any form is said to degrade man's soul: "The expense of spirit in a waste of shame /Is lust in action… Savage, extreme, rude, cruel, not to trust; / Enjoyed no sooner but despised straight; / Past reason hunted; and no sooner had, / Past reason hated, as a swallowed bait, / On purpose laid to make the taker made"?

Gorey was one of those bachelor-dilettantes towards whom Edith Wharton was always drawn, a man – like her friends Walter Berry and Egerton Winthrop – who preferred to live in a private world of his own, standing aside from the general press. He was tall, big-limbed – Oscar Wilde, who also loved furred clothes, was 6'3" – and frequently depicted himself in his drawings as a tall, ungainly, bearded figure, generally leaning off-true while holding something like a croquet mallet. This figure, often wearing a huge turtle-necked cardigan, appears over and over in his many books. They are invariably never fathers. I believe that the very idea of living with another person would have become abhorrent to Gorey. A wife? Children? They would have gotten in his way. *Consequences* would have gotten in his way. Consequences did. I have mentioned Henry James. In James's wonderful story, "The Lesson of the Master," an older writer warns a younger one against the "idols of the market place," among which, strange to say, he quite blithely numbers such inconveniences as "placing one's children and dressing one's wife." However, for the lover of the beautiful and the perfect, "marriage interferes," the master counsels. James himself never risked the possibility of that blunder and was consistently ill-disposed to do so. "I am too good a bachelor to spoil," he once confided to a friend.

Anton Chekhov declared, "If you're afraid of loneliness, don't marry." I think it may sum up an Edward Gorey paraphobia.

L et it be understood that although they shared certain characteristics he was not decadent, nothing like, say, the fussily gay and priggish bon-vivant of the Thirties, Lucius Beebe, author, railroad maven, prankster – he once gaily festooned financier J.P. Morgan's yacht "Corsair" with toilet paper from a chartered plane – and dedicated gourmand who was proudly a member of the *Confrérie des Chevaliers du Tastevin*. ("A gourmet can tell from the flavor whether a woodcock's leg is the one on which the bird is accustomed to roost," he once declared.) A clothes horse who wore only bespoke tailoring, Beebe's coats were mink *lined*. It was even his custom to appear in college classes wearing a monocle and gold-handled cane. He wrote a column for the *New York Herald Tribune* chronicling the doings of fashionable society at such storied restaurants as the El Morocco and the Stork Club. Later in life, he owned two personal railroad cars. Like Gorey, "Luscious Lucius," as he was called, went to Harvard, collected books, loved fur, reviewed movies – in his case, he also had a lifelong companion, one Charles Clegg, later a suicide – but whereas Beebe was a wastrel, an egoist, and a flâneur who saw to it that he dined at the best restaurants in the world ("Throw wide the windows! Air out the rooms!" he once howled upon seeing a row of orchids at his table. "Must the bouquet of my wines conflict with these stinking flowers?"), Gorey's life was not only gentle and quiet but compassionate and chaste – virtually a *vita angelica* – and basically an unvarious one spent in a quiet residence.

I have often wondered when considering Gorey's lack of social or emotional commitment whether he did not have a strong feeling for a difficult but fascinating woman named Violet Ranney ("Bunny") Lang back in his old

Violet Ranney ("Bunny") Lang.

Harvard days. They were certainly close. V.R. Lang (1924-1956), a sort of "Our Lady of the Poets' Theater," was a big outgoing blonde, a well-born but tough Bostonian and somewhat petulant eccentric, or, in Alison Lurie's words, "a feminist before the movement was reinvented in the dark ages of the early 1950s." Bunny married Bradley Sawyer Phillips who was the son of Dr. Philip Phillips, the curator of North American Archaeology at Harvard's Peabody Museum. Their wedding ceremony at Christ Church in Cambridge was noted in the *New York Times* of April 16, 1955. In 1975, Lurie published a sort of love/hate memoir of Bunny Lang as a preface to a Random House edition of Lang's poems and plays. This was a reissue of an earlier privately printed paperback, *The Pitch* (1962), which featured a not very well-done, and so rare, Gorey dust-jacket along with several of his funereal illustrations. An irreverent, energetic, devil-may-care young woman with dyed hair and no end of a kind of desperate bravado, Lang raced through life, often wore thrift-shop clothes, and kept cantankerous friendships with the likes of James Merrill, John Ashbery, Kenneth Koch, Gorey's Harvard room-mate Frank O'Hara, and of course Gorey himself. Although she was a "nice Boston girl" who lived in a distinguished four-story brownstone at 209 Bay State Road in the sedate part of Boston's Back Bay, Bunny was something of a genuine Holly Golightly figure who threw lavish birthday parties for herself, acted on stage, once or twice even stripped in the chorus line at the Old Howard Burlesque House on seedy Hanover St., and along with fiery plays wrote strong poems with such wonderful lines as

> *Love you, love you I do! Love you!*
> *Ham, shank and shoulders, lights too.*

and

> *Why is your dark like a bag with a man in it?*
> *In the moment of panic, hardly anything happens,*
> *But nothing is true. I remember, I knew.*

She wore odd clothes, drank heavily, and told people the truth to their faces. She wrote plays and in them named villainesses after herself and often played the roles. To revenge herself on a man she didn't like, she had thousands of pink labels printed, proclaiming "My name is Parker and I am a pig," and pasted them up all over the wretched man's neighborhood. On a smaller scale she wished her cat off on a devoted friend whose inability to say no reduced her life to a shamble dominated by guilt, rage, the cat, and a litter of kittens. It sometimes seems that the vapidity of her friends' lives alone made Bunny's friendship worth the price she exacted. A friend of hers, Sallie Bingham wrote in 1975:

> People were addicted to her opinion of them; she seemed to stamp her followers with her own authenticity. She was a special kind of woman – one who combined great literary talent with great organizational ability, driving energy and a gift for publicity. She once wrote, directed and starred in her own play. Her 'angry loyalty' to friends and lovers helped, of course; the absolute social security of her background was perhaps even more important. Bunny had grown up in a society so small and stable that to give someone's name was sufficient description. She was unique only in that she extended this rule to people from outside this society.

Somebody at a party once asked Bunny, "What do you do?" Lang replied,

> What do I like? Well, let's see. I wake up about noon; I have breakfast in bed, and I read magazines and the papers, and then I write letters or something. Then about four I get up and have a lovely long bath and dress and go and have cocktails with friends at the Ritz, or they come to my house or I go to theirs; then dinner somewhere; and then, if I'm not going out that evening, I come home and read a novel, or maybe I play old records over.

Bunny Lang died absurdly young, of cancer, burning out at the age of 32, having lived like so many such doomed people as if she knew that her allotted time was limited. Although Lurie wrote, "To be with Bunny was like alcohol: at first exhilarating, but in the end destructive." I cannot confess to being privy to anything in this matter, but I have always known that Bunny Lang, to whom Gorey dedicated *The Hapless Child*, was an extremely special soul to him, and who knows, maybe more than that, someone he loved but whose untimely death took part of him away. Gorey was not particularly at ease with women. I do know, however, that he was capable of great adoration, truly Stendhalian in power – art truly moved him – and over the years he was explicitly devoted to such great prima ballerinas as Patricia McBride, Maria Calegari, Suzanne Farrell, and, among others, to Diana Adams, to whom he dedicated *The Gilded Bat* (1967), and especially to Allegra Kent ("I have always worshipped at her shrine") who once telephoned him in New York (he almost fainted, he told me) to invite him to a private party for which Gorey happily contributed one of his brilliant drawings. I recall once going on at length about Carmelita Maracci, the lovely ballerina who so beautifully performed Tereza's (Claire Bloom's) dances in *Limelight (*1952), but I'm not certain that my commendation registered with Gorey as true passion. He might have thought it was borrowed apocalypse. Possibly he felt I had not seen enough of ballerinas to judge. I don't know, maybe he agreed.

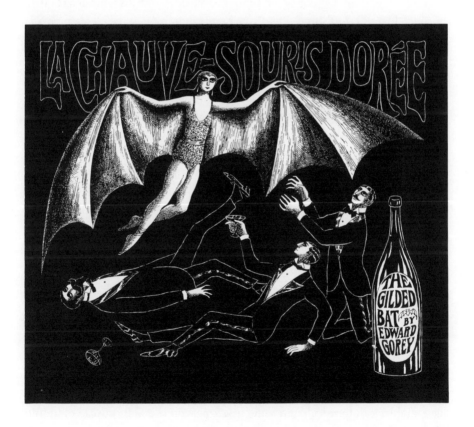

From *The Gilded Bat.*

Gorey was shy, private, and, a lot like Sherlock Holmes who knew everything about such exotica as varieties of tobacco ash and English soil but not, say, the carfare to Catford or Maida Vale or Hempstead, bored by certain, mostly practical subjects that singularly failed to interest him, like the best way to Athol or why local eggs are brown or the cost of a beach sticker on Cape Cod. On the other hand, he could discuss for hours – for entire *days* – the films of Feuillade or French surrealism or Franju's *Judex* or Federico Fellini's *Nights of Cabiria* or the novels of Ivy Compton-Burnette or 19th-century book illustration or the paintings of Goya, whom he loved. I do know that unless something intrigued him he generally had to rise to the occasion to respond to it. "Life is intrinsically, well, boring and dangerous at the same time," he once said. "At any given moment the floor may open up. Of course, it almost never does – that's what makes it so boring." His standoffishness vividly came through in an appearance he made in 1997 on the *Dick Cavett Show*, which was pretty much of a disaster. With his characteristically pretentious and intrusive self-importance – those prissy Yale witticisms – Cavett, right in his element, was clearly trying to score off his unassuming and visibly uneasy guest from the very first moment with the farcical banter he presumptuously assumed an original, thoughtful man like Gorey would expect. Gorey, out of shock, I suspect, but maybe disgust, was virtually mute. He gave one-word answers, nettled replies. A public forum was not anything he enjoyed. Quipping with fools or professional girdle-salesmen was certainly not what he was about. "I see," he invariably said softly as the dry, gloomy response offered to anyone feeding him a line or trying to cozen him. "I was under the impression that this was leading somewhere."

Edward Gorey was never one thing. I would watch him make up his mind as to which Gorey to enact – erudite, courteous, silly, disobedient, prevaricating, fake-morbid for fun in photos. He could be elated, jabberwocking, fretting, glum, never not glum. I have seen him many, many times sober, his face drawn white with intensity. Remember it was Jonathan Swift who, although he was the inventor of the phrase "sweetness and light," is now reputed to be one of the embittered misanthropes of history. Thomas Hobbes, the philosopher, at the age of ninety went about singing to strengthen his lungs and prolong his life. William Morris, who always did his creative work behind a curtain, refused to have a tablecloth for meals and hung his carpets on the walls instead of on the floor. Leo Tolstoy who humbly felt he was undeserving of his inherited wealth and gave away money to peasants, dispensing large sums of money to street beggars while on trips to the city, much to his wife's chagrin, and stopped his creative work because of a religious call, was excommunicated from the church by the Holy Synod of Russia and derided and pointed at by louts who shouted at him, "Look! There goes the devil in human form!" George Bernard Shaw ate only tomatoes and brown bread, was happiest in cold weather, hated his first name, out of a compulsive habit wore only tweedy Norfolk jackets and knickerbockers, refused social meals ("I find that eating gets in the way of sociability. One can never talk when one eats"), considered Chekhov a greater dramatist than Shakespeare, and always insisted that his plays were essentially poetic dramas that should be sung. As the late Joe Orton said in *What the Butler Saw*, "You can't be a rationalist in an irrational world."

No, Gorey was eccentric, there is no question. Who are you acquainted with, for instance, who has read all of Trollope, all 17 novels, *all 47 books*, but would not miss a single episode of TV's *All My Children* or Andy Griffith in reruns of *Matlock*? Read Lao-tse with understanding but collected true crime magazines and loved *Doctor Who*, that improbable science fiction TV series? Cherished Oliver Onions, but watched *The Mary Tyler Moore Show* episodes and collected current videos? Could speak with total authority on the novels of Theodore Dreiser or Yukio Mishima and yet was word-perfect on the films of English actress Pamela Franklin and could quote chapter and verse from the 1958 film, *Fiend Without a Face*, in which a scientist materializes thoughts in the form of invisible brain-shaped creatures which kill people for food? Sat up dutifully by himself to watch movies virtually every night?

As I have said, Gorey loved movies. In fact he once did weekly movie-reviews for *Soho Weekly* under the pseudonym "Wardore Edgy," a name compilers of his anagrammatic names always miss. He often referred in various interviews to the fact of his parents having taken him to movies very early in life. Great films were shown at the Brattle Theater during his Harvard years. And there were decade-long periods in New York City when he and friends would go to see, as he said, a "thousand movies a year." On Christmas Day in Manhattan for the longest time, in order to stifle the oppression of a holiday he claimed he could not stand, Gorey would begin in the morning, either with friends or alone, and then pass the day consecutively watching four or five full-length movies without a break. I do know that he had a weakness for "sinister cinema" retrospectives and distinctly recall him telling me that over dull holiday weekends in Manhattan he would go to Jessie Matthew Festivals showing *It's Love Again, Sailing Along*, and *The Good Companion* as

EG in his late 20s at Freezer Rd. House, Barnstable, Cape Cod.

well as Harold Lloyd Festivals where he saw hard-to-find early Lloyd movies like *Dr. Jack* or *Grandma's Boy,* Lloyd's first feature-length film from 1922. "I have seen much archival stuff," he told Annie Nocenti in a 1998 interview for *Scenario: The Magazine of Screenwriting Art.* "Many years ago the Museum of Modern Art ran off their entire archive on Saturday morning for years on end, and a bunch of us would go up there, into their tiny screening room, and we watched everything they had." I know he also tried to see any cult films he could and more than once mentioned *Twisted Creeps*; *Blood and Donuts*; *Creation of the Humanoids*; even a thing called *Pubes in Phallusland*!

Rather than discuss his own work, he much preferred to talk with me about movies: Louise Fazenda in *Wonder Bar* (1934) and Jimmy Fidler in *Garden of the Moon* (1938) and Baby Quintanilla in *Forty Little Mothers* (1940) and Walter Pidgeon in *Million Dollar Mermaid* (1952). He saw virtually every motion picture from *Amaryllis of Clothes-Line Alley* (1918) to *Amarcord* (1974) to *Arachnophobia* (1991). I remember that he enjoyed Louis Malle's *Au Revoir, Les Enfants* which I also liked and personally found particularly poignant, as I myself once suffered from the same indisposition, the bed-wetting scene where Julien is mocked by the other boys at what I believe was St. Croix, the exclusive Carmelite boarding school in the Île-de-France. He loved Fu Manchu movies, Charlie Chan, the *Thin Man* series, and *The Perils of Pauline*. He was word-perfect about the silents and was widely familiar with early Hollywood and could cite the éclat of long out-of-date actors and actresses, people like Hugh Herbert, Verree Teasdale, Reginald Owen, Walter Catlett, Estelle Winwood, Rex Caldwell, Frank McHugh, Aubrey Smith, ZaSu Pitts, and "dahling" Tallulah Bankhead in her Wanda Myro phase, "the fake Serbian princess." He knew how early films were made and where and who on the sets was bonking whom. Small things were not lost on him, and he had opinions on everything from John Boles's mustache to Jane Darwell's dewlaps to Jerry Colonna's eyes. Said Gorey, reflecting on the dear old days of early cinema, "I have seen endless numbers of silent films. Many of those D.W. Griffith two-reelers are gems. Charlie Chaplin was without a doubt the greatest comedian, but my idols are Buster Keaton and of course Bea Lillie, the funniest woman who ever lived. Have you seen her in *On Approval*? 1931, I think. Or in *Exit Smiling*, MGM 1926? It's as nearly perfect a comedy as I have ever seen. I really do think movies made a terrible mistake when they started to talk, for the most part. The imagination was engaged, you know? What has killed movies to my mind are the special effects. See one screen filled with flames, and you have seen all of them." Characteristically, one of Gorey's Soho reviews snidely began, "Young man overheard saying to his girlfriend around NYU: 'Make a movie of it, Roseanne, and shove it up your ass.' It is this sensibility, I feel, that accounts for so much of the film-making today."

One of Gorey's favorite actresses was Tuesday Weld, and at one point back in the 1990s I remember him enthusiastically suggesting that a "Tuesday Weld Film Festival" be held where one could view such inimitable screen gems as *Pretty Poison* with stork-shouldered Tony Perkins – along with the famous deleted scene! – *Lord Love a Duck, Wild in the Country, The Cincinnati Kid, Thief,* and *Looking for Mr. Goodbar.* I believe that the pressures of her career, resulting in a nervous breakdown at age nine, alcoholism by age 12, and a suicide attempt around the same time all served to endear her to the artist.

As we see, Gorey was not locked into watching top-flight films exclusively or approving only the best movies. He loved to see ground-level nightmare and horror movies, both national and international, films passionate thrillkillerites especially love, like *Suspiria* (1977) and *The Town That Dreaded Sundown* (1977) and *Women of Straw* (1964). I believe that the definite Gorey movie *qua* movie, one that he loved, of course, as do I, but also one that regarding plot, settings, themes, imagery, etc. could literally have comprised one of his very own books – an archetypal one – is the spooky comic classic, *The Bat Whispers*, directed in 1930 by Roland West, who incidentally had a long affair with the doomed Thelma Todd, in whose still unsolved, mysterious death he might very well have been involved. It is an early "talkie" version of *The Bat,* the Broadway hit of 1920 by Mary Roberts Rinehart and Avery Hopwood which tells the story of odd people exploring an old mansion looking for a hidden treasure while a caped killer picks them off one by one. It has all the kitsch, lightning and thunder, scary paintings with moving eyes, a skeleton-in-armor, hidden rooms, slate roofs, endless staircases with newel posts the size of the Bunker Hill monument, and "enough shrubbery around the grounds to hide a dozen assassins." All the sets, I mean, are pure Gorey. Guns go off! A bat-clothed man goes ripping about! The photography is brilliant. There is no end of group lunacy. Wealthy, tubby Cornelia van Gorder (Grayce Hampton) with her cane and shawl and her pretty niece, Dale (Una Merkel) with shingled hair "engaged to a runaway cashier." Dr. Venrees with his Transylvanian accent. Be-derbied Charles Dow Clark as "Detective W.T. Jones, super sleuth of Oakdale County," who couldn't find a clue if it were sitting on his lap, and of course The Bat who cries out at the end, "I've got the greatest brain that ever existed!" I have seen

EG's *Tragic Secrets* and *Heads Will Roll & Wallpaper* were first performed in 1996.

the movie many times and still insist that the silly, hysterical maid, Lizzie Allen (Maude Eburne), steals the entire show, squeaking and squealing around in her fat pajamas with spiderweb designs (!), howling at every noise! At the end the creepy Detective Anderson (Chester Morris) proclaims, "The bat always flies at night and in a straight line!"

B-movies are in such short supply that when one turns up, it should be potentially treasured on that account," wrote Gorey in a 1974 review of *Sugar Hill*, a voodoo-revenge blaxploitation film involving zombies conjured out of the grave. "It's all very badly done but in a genial, unprepossessing way, and one of the charms of the movie is being able to redo it so much better in one's head." *Redo it in one's head.* It is a revealing phrase, I think. Much in the way of what Gorey observed, I feel, *was* redone in his head – I mean, in the sense that he was madly unpredictable and astonishingly prone by way of counter-thought to go against prevailing opinion and perfectly prepared to set things in his thinkball. He constantly redid in his mind what in most people's brains was not even half done.

Reverse-snobbery is one explanation. It is the quirk of "camp," the antic, some say predominantly gay-oriented topsyturvification of aesthetic values. *Kitschkultur.* Love of send-up. All that. But just when one would think that Gorey was *the* anti-bourgeois moviegoer of all time and so insistently avant-garde, he would surprise you. Gorey always claimed with a straight face, for example, that not only were John Wayne and William Shatner good actors – *hello?* – but that Charlton Heston was "the actor of our time." Mel Brooks to his critical eye was not just an oafish and colossal bore; with his tastelessness he actually *offended* Gorey who in a 1972 review called his widely acclaimed *The Producers* (1968), "The most offensive movie I ever saw," antiphonally adding as a stinging coda, "I've now seen *Blazing Saddles*, and I no longer think this." Simply, Gorey did not get in line. Gene Hackman – his every performance – Gorey described as "suet." He told me that he could tolerate a good western, if it was intelligible. "But take the Burts," he once went on to say, "Burt Lancaster in *Apache* playing Massai, the last Apache warrior, wasn't bad, I guess – his devoted blue-eyed squaw, Jean Peters from Canton, Ohio, how do you do, hung onto her man like Saran Wrap, but I gotta tell ya that Burt Reynolds in the lead role of *Navajo Joe*, a turkey with full wattles filmed in Spain with Italian actors about the American West, made me want to hurl my box of popcorn at the screen!" Of the comedian Steve Martin, he wrote, "I find someone like him physically repellent in some inexplicable way." Gorey could be hilarious, of course, and wonderfully, endlessly uncharitable. Sam Waterston "looks like the offspring of Roddy McDowall and Tony Perkins." TV's *Cheers* star Ted Danson, Gorey once told me he thought looked "Frankensteinian." He dismissed Robert Redford as "hero-needy." ("It is fatal for an actor to have an image of himself," he said) Actress Regina Baff, who appears in *The Great Gatsby*, a movie Gorey panned, "looks like a disemboweled mattress." I forget who it was – Cher, I think – whom he described as "dull as a box of cornflakes." Director Sidney Lumet he called "Frank Perry with knobs on." Robert Altman Gorey dismissed as a total bore. "He seems not so much to make movies, as not to make other ones. With *Thieves Like Us,* he is not making *You Only Live Once, They Live By Night,* and *Bonnie and Clyde,* to name those that easily come to mind. Each of Mr. Altman's films is directed within an inch of its feeble little life, seemingly to no other purpose than to show that it has been."

I once had the chance to read Gorey's amazing screenplay for *The Black Doll,* the original 1973 text of 50-plus pages, an astonishingly dense script, all text, with quick, ominous postcard-short scenes about a "priceless ritual object" (PRO), excavated in central Asia by Prof. Horace Bedsock and then stolen, which leads to all sort of surrealistic intrigues and adventures. Werner Herzog was Gorey's first choice to direct it, "although," he quipped, "I don't think his sense of humor is exactly there." He also mentioned as other possible directors Lars Von Trier; French director Francis Girod (*The Internal Trio*), Jean Pierre Mocky, who "made a film about someone stealing from poor-boxes in churches" – even Stephan Elliott, whose outrageous and highly campy movie *The Adventures of Priscilla, Queen of the Desert* remained a distinct Gorey favorite.

Gorey, as we have seen, had strong opinions but never moreso than when talking about the world of movies, actors, and movie-lore. "*L.A. Confidential* was close to thirty minutes too long." "*Body Heat,* which has about seventy-five endings, made me want to stomp out of the theatre, folks – like about seventy-five times!" "Streisand's *Funny Girl* is of course the low-water mark in all of Twentieth-Century culture." "I would rather stare at an African bead for a fortnight than have to see Richard Dreyfuss in another film!" "No one cannot watch *I Love You Again* forty times in a row." "Young Bette Davis in *Fashions of 1934* is of course one of the great matchless Bette Davises." "Who among the hopeless ingenues nowadays can possibly surpass petite Laura La

PRESENTED BY THE COTUIT CENTER FOR THE ARTS
DIRECTED BY CAROL VERBURG · ORIGINAL SCORE
BY JAMES WOLF · SET BY EDWARD GOREY
8:00 PM FRIDAY & SATURDAY MAY 2·3, 9·10, 16·17, 23·24
SUNDAY MAY 18 & 25 · 737 MAIN ST(ANNEX) COTUIT
TICKETS $10   RESERVATIONS (508) 428·0669

EG's *Hamlet* was first performed in 1997.

Plante with her shingled hairdo in *The Cat and the Canary*?" "I loved Donna Reed in *The Far Horizons* making fry bread in her couture buckskin designed by Edith Head – at least her dyed black wig didn't drop off into the Snake River!" "Whatever happened to Lya DePutti? I haven't seen her in yonks!" Gorey loved the usual stars, of course: Marlene Dietrich, Judy Garland, Bette Davis, Ingrid Bergman, and Myrna Loy. I remember him telling me of his affection for Marilyn Monroe after reading that, when married to James Dougherty, she once tried to drag a cow out of the rain and into the house. ("I'm so glad to meet the president of India," she gushed in 1956, squeezing the hand of Sukarno, president of Indonesia.) He also adored Isabelle Adjani, the dark-eyed Delphine Seyrig of *Last Year at Marienbad*; and, as I recall, the meltingly lovely, soul-harrowingly beautiful Louise Brooks, my own personal candidate for the ultimate ravishing beauty of the cinema, I don't care what era. I have heard Gorey hold court many times with astonishing *savoir faire* in discussions of the hair-styles of actresses and what they meant to him. Fatigue – on any subject, hair, movies, books, actors, and actresses, whatever – simplified his judgments. Then, everything he liked was "to die for," while everything he disliked was "the pits."

No film was too out of the way, too out of fashion, or too old. He loved *Pimple's Midsummer Night's Dream* – after eating a lobster, Pimple suffers from a nightmare about cannibals! – *La Llorona*, *The Wax Lady, King Klunk, The Electric Vitalizer,* and *Zambo the Ape-Man*. "I probably could not stand meeting Vilma Banky or Mabel Normand in real life, but silverized on a screen 40 feet high, and 20 feet wide? Scrumpy!"

"My favorite thriller of all time is *The Lady Vanishes*," Gorey once pronounced with finality. He agreed with me that Henri-Georges Clouzot's *Diabolique* was the "most terrifying movie of all time," and he insisted that every director plagiarized from it. I recall once having a great discussion with Gorey about the sociologically diagnostic aspects of 1940s *Blondie* movies, starring Penny Singleton and Arthur Lake, which we both loved and could discuss in depth. What buoyancy one feels in hearing someone talk about, not the same tired old flicks, but Billie Dove in *Blondie of the Follies* and Buster Keaton in *The General* and *Lady and the Master* (1944) and *Belle Le Grand* (1951) starring the Czech ex-skater Vera Hruba Ralston! I was pleased that, taking all things into consideration, Gorey agreed with me that Buster Keaton was the greatest film comic of all time. Maybe even the greatest director!

The Saphead! Sherlock, Jr.! College! Steamboat Bill, Jr.! We concurred that W. C. Fields was also matchless and right up there with him. Once or twice I was truly amazed at Gorey's inexplicable taste – or lack of it! I remember him saying, "*Star Wars* is very important," a film (and its sequels) I myself considered not so much Hollywood trash as a fat, inconsequential farce of ersatz theology and simpleminded New Age bollocks all cobbled together out of a thousand filched sources, including ancient Greek fable, Buck Rogers movies, naval jumpsuits, Japanese samurai swords, mempo masks, World War I German blaster guns, oversimplified "evil empire" fables, Nazi myths, fascist uniforms, quest literature, and, I'm convinced, Xerxes of the Persian Wars marching down through Thessaly to Salamis! Except, of course, that *those* were interesting! I love musicals and especially the music to *Brigadoon* and *Paint Your Wagon,* but Gorey refused my praise of the movies made of them ("A chinstrap penguin could tell those were fake sets from Hell!"), but he allowed me to love *Show Boat,* the cast of which he could do no end of amusing imitations, Julie, Gaylord, Magnolia, Cap'n Andy, Parthy Ann, and – I *promise*! – little Kim! Gorey treasured standards like Fritz Lang's *Metropolis*, F. W. Murnau's *Sunrise*, Peter Lorre in *M*, all the Busby Berkeley *Gold Digger* films, and most things campy and excessive and disreputable. "Oh, and of course *Mädchen in Uniform*. Now that's a zippy movie! I adore anything with a kitten and a whip!"

All of Gorey's books resonate with the subjects, plots, entire vocabulary – and *feel* – of Twenties and Thirties cinema; lost love, willful debutantes, pashas and Egyptian daggers, Gardens of Allah, beaded curtains, mysterious dolls, fables of stage, detective and mystery, innocent children. Any serious reader of his simply knows that much of his vision has grown out of cinematic gems like *Stamboul Quest, Union Pacific, Morocco, The Thirty-Nine Steps*, and things like *Mr. Moto's Last Warning*. He had as an astonishing feel for the curve of a story – the right scene, the exact word, the certain atmosphere, the suitable name, the correct mood, the perfect title – as any Hollywood director did.

Given to hyperbole, full of perception, insightful and not afraid to be critical, he preferred talking about movies than any other subject on earth. "The first [Louis] Feuillade I saw," he told Nocenti, "were the fragments left of *Fantômas*. I saw *Tih Minh* and *Les Vampires* and of course *Barrabas*, which I think is the greatest movie ever made." Superlatives flow. "*A Countess from Hong Kong*, Chaplin's last movie, I think is one of the greatest movies ever made, and I'm the only person I know who thinks that," he said. "I suppose

Limelight is much too long, but I love his few scenes with Keaton and of course that moment when he says, 'We are all amateurs. We don't live long enough to be anything else.'" "I still insist that Ava Gardner in *She Went to the Races,* at 23, was at her prettiest." "Who doesn't love Linda Darnell in *Forever Amber*? In my opinion she took extreme closeups as triumphantly as any other actress on film." "There's a movie I'm dying to see again – Jacques Tourneur's *The Curse of the Demon*. It's a great horror movie, from a story by M.R. James, who does very cozy but very scary ghost stories, which I do not read before I go to bed." Great. Worst. Greater. The dimmest…

Gorey always exaggerated to make a point. It was far less a way of getting one to listen, at least as far as I'm concerned, than a means of liking something a lot, or better; it usually managed to accomplish both. Hyperbole underlined things for him in a sense and reinforced his point. It was also completely bound up with his passion. I have heard him many times refer to a hundred different movies as "the greatest movie ever made." But then who on earth would expect consistency of a fellow who could state in a single monologue, "I'm very fond of *Buffy, the Vampire Slayer*" while making the co-pronouncement, "You could offer me a Bernini or a Canova, and I'd say, 'Oh, take it away, please'?" Extravagance of opinion was a way for him of insisting and I suspect was used the way the writer Flannery O'Connor said she used the grotesque the way she did, because people are deaf and dumb and need help to see and hear.

The art of creative deflation – wittily – amused him. "The Dolly Sisters, Rosie and Jenny? Rosika and Jansci Deutsch from Big Nose, Budapest! – I won't tell if you don't." "Dark seductress of the silents, Rosemary Theby, she of *The Reincarnation of Karma* and *Dice of Destiny* and *The Mystery of 13*, never put her hats on straight!" "I can't quite decide who gets my vote to play Clytemnestra – Olive Hasbrouck in *Dog Biscuits,* Bethel Leslie in *Time of the Cuckoo,* or Louise Allbritton, the tragic Sybil Hale in *They Won't Forget*." "Ann Revere, merely *standing* there, gave me the fantods!" "Didn't our friend Fatty Arbuckle end up in a hotel room drinking tequila like a Jalisco mariachi?" "I dreamt I went on TV's *The Dating Game* and my only choices – *ouch*! –were Ethel Griffies, Marjorie Main, and Zeffie Tilbury." "Susan Hayward – born Edythe Marrener? The poor dear badly needed to go scream at the landscape for an afternoon as a Reichian exercise in self-contact!" "Horse-faced Ann Revere does not speak, she intones, "I cannot quite manage

The Cotuit Center for the Arts
presents a
Family Entertainment

CAUTIONARY TALES FOR CHILDREN

by Hilaire Belloc

With the puppets of
Le Théâtricule stoïque
directed by Edward Gorey

Saturdays at 8:00 PM & Sundays at 5:30 PM
October 26, 27, November 2, 3
Halloween at 8:00 PM

Admission $5
Reservations
(508) 428·0669

EG's *Cautionary Tales for Children* was first performed in 1989.

Anthony Quinn in that annoying growl-a-minute, testosterone-driven persona of his later years – please spare me!" "Adele Jergens at her trashiest redeemed *Armored Car Robbery* for me, which featured every just about every character actor *who ever lived*: Charles McGraw, Steve Brodie, William Talman – *Perry Mason*'s Hamilton Berger! – Douglas Fowley, Gene Evans. It takes me back to the 1950s and early dreams like no magic carpet could!" "Al Pacino in *Godfather III*, I'm sorry, kids, walked through that awful part looking just like Stan Laurel! – the word for that performance is *épouvantable* – and, God forgive me, was Eli Wallach in that same film actually *trying* to channel Kukla, Fran, and Ollie?" "Robert Taylor? – eek! Preposterous lumpfish! He sang for HUAC but always talked too much! Didn't he actually state in *Knights of the Round Table* that he wanted *to sleep with his horse*?" In *Bedlam*, the matchless Boris Karloff, poor dear, had to wear shaped wigs that resembled licorice!"

I recall that he liked "list" discussion, as did I. He once began for no particular reason I saw enumerating celebrities with widow's peaks – Dick Powell, Robert Taylor, Marilyn Monroe, etc. Did he attach importance to them? Not particularly. *Observation* was the point. He liked the way Humphrey Bogart said "Thursby" and the way Robert Newton said "Jim 'Arkins" and the way Audrey Hepburn said "chocolate" and the way unshaven Akim Tamiroff said "Drunken bum – I should shoot you in the *fooooot*." Another time we got into an assessment of legs in cinema. We dismissed the "shortpins" group right off as unsalvageable – Alan Ladd, Al Pacino, Tom Cruise, Mario Lanza, Dudley Moore. Gorey maintained that the goofy actor Dustin Hoffman was not only a midget but had something of a tic-toc walk, insisting that in a hideously unprepossessing way he "tottered" or lurched, resembling a hideous wind-up toy. I said that John Wayne listed as he walked, appearing always off-true. Height played a role in that, we agreed. I said something was wrong in that department with Charlton Heston, that if you concentrate on his legs in *The Ten Commandments* or *Ben-Hur* – it is seen best when he is bare-legged – you can't help but notice his odd leg/walk configuration. I knew that Ted had a weak spot for sci-fi films and city-ravaging creatures, the loonier the better. I remember once challenging him to tell me how each of the following monster films the creatures were dispatched: *The Blob*; *The Beast of Hollow Mountain*; *Rodan, the Flying Monster*; *Them!*; *The Beast from 20,000 Fathoms*; *The Deadly Mantis*; *Invasion of the Saucermen*; and *The Fly*, and he nailed every one – frozen; quicksand; lava; burned to death by flamethrowers; shot in the throat with radioactive isotopes; gassed with cyanide bombs; dissolved by high-intensity auto headlight beams; and of course crushed by a hydraulic press and eaten by a spider, respectively.

He was a virtual expert on foreign films. As we have seen, he loved the work of Feuillade, the silent filmmaker of the early 1900s. "Top of my list for movies I'd like to see before I die are any of the Feuillades I haven't seen, and I haven't seen all that many. My favorite horror movie is Franju's *Eyes Without a Face*," said Gorey. "As I say, I love *Diabolique*. Then there's this one Clouzot, one of the great goofy movies ever made, called *La Prisonnière*, I think it was the only movie he made in color. It all takes place in a kind of arty milieu, so that the color is very Mondrian – dead white and then bright blue, bright red, bright yellow, and black. Another great influence on me, in an idiotic way, was an Italian serial called *Gray Rats*." Films, he made no secret of saying, influenced him in his own books. He repeated that director Fritz Lang was one of the major influences on his own art. He often referred to Jetta Goudal in *The Forbidden Women* and Claire Windsor on *The Eternal 3* and not without pity to Eva Tanguay, the "I Don't Care Girl" of Vaudeville, who, he always added by way of exequy, "died alone on a remote street in a small Hollywood cottage." How did he know so much about their deaths? What memory file in what room in Gorey's mind could keep straight after so many years all the facts about sextress Barbara La Marr that he could tell me, after she drank herself to death on January 30, 1926, she had been laid out in a rose-colored casket at the Walter C. Blue Undertaking Chapel, lying in state for three days while 65,000 passed by to see her?

I was always struck by how many character actors lived in captivity inside Edward Gorey's head, from childhood, I gather – people like Sig Rumann, Douglass Dumbrille, morbid-faced George Zucco, Jack Ingram, Una Merkel, Tim McCoy, Adele Mara, Howard da Silva, Mae Busch, fat Laird Cregar, Rex Bell, James Millican – "He acted in every movie that ever was!" Ted would announce. "Count 'em, folks!" – Eric Christmas, the "villainous" Ray Barcroft, and Max Terhune, the cowboy sidekick, among others. I was impressed with the way they almost seemed to be friends of his. He could count off without hesitation all of the actors who had played Red Ryder: Allan "Rocky" Lane, Jim Bannon, Don "Red" Barry, and "Wild Bill" Elliot. I can still remember him saying with a mild-mannered but irresistible spoof, "I cannot decide which Rochelle Hudson film I want to take to my desert island, *Girl Crazy*, *Fanny Foley Herself*, or *The Penguin Pool Murder*, in which she plays a telephone operator more cunning than a bisset!" Gorey's many stories had their perfect match in the intrigue I have always had for the creative and the crackpated. I remember telling Ted that my very first television experience was watching the phantasmagorical *The Phantom Empire* ("The Most Astounding Serial Ever Made"), starring my hero Gene Autry, the "Singing Cowboy," a vivid 12-episode 1935 Mascot serial that combined the western, musical, and science fiction genres. I would sit transfixed watching with my neighborhood friends on a big old RCA console way back in 1949 the underground empire of Murania, complete with towering skyscrapers, robots, ray-guns, elevators tubes that extend miles from the surface, and an icy, evil blonde Queen Tika – sexy to me at age 10, although it was cute little Betsy King Ross on whom I had my real crush, a little spring-ghost of a teen with blunt-cut hair who was very likely the first girl I ever loved. On the surface, a group of crooks under Prof. Beetson plan to invade Murania and seize its radium wealth, while in Murania, a group of revolutionaries plot to overthrow Queen Tika. The Thunder Guards who made a rumbling thunder sound when they rode – the neo-Wagnerian music accompanying them matched their Prussianesque helmets – were terrifying and always emerged like gypsy moths onto the surface world from a mysterious cave where a huge rock door opened, then closed, remindful of Ali Baba. Both Muranians and Prof. Beetson's team want to get rid of Autry. This cave impressed me more than anything. As a macabre and almost diabolical image, it gripped me with the same mysterious fascination that Gorey's work would so many years later.

G orey did not smoke, wore a ring in his right ear – later, both ears – loved to wear pendants, was passionately devoted to Mozart, Schubert and Bach (he had 500 CDs of Bach), and as a small hobby-cum-fixation (usually while watching soap operas from one p.m. to four p.m.) was given to making – *hand-sewing each one*! – beanbag frogs. Beanbag frogs! He especially loved Handel's "Messiah" and collected versions of it. When he was once asked who his favorite composer was, he answered, "Telemann." Make of it what you will. Was this the music he happened to be listening to that week? Entirely possible. He harbored more than a slumbering passion for the art of topiary. Topiary figures everywhere in works of his, such as, for example, *The Improvable Landscape, Leaves from a Mislaid Album, Tragédies Topiares, The Dwindling Party,* and *Les Échanges Malandreux.* The configurations are limitless. Hedge-art. Again, shapes of every kind intrigued him. Urns – for ashes, cremation, plants, memorials, or simple decoration – serve as a recurrent image in many Gorey stories, and no better example can be found than in his *Les Urnes Utiles* (1980), evoking dread and menace. Stone walls also held a fascination for him but only the kind fashioned with cobblestone-sized boulders and then those neatly arranged. (A perfect Gorey wall of just that sort can be seen below the late 17th century graveyard on the right-hand side driving down his old street, Millway, in Barnstable.) There is a plethora in his work, as well, of divans, iron railings, bicycles, insects, furs – *The Water Flowers* is, among other things, a paean to the fur coat – umbrellas, wheelchairs, stalagmites, and stalagtites. The dark thematic underbelly of existence, mined so well by Alfred Hitchcock in his films, the bleakness of humanity, was always saved by Gorey's unrelenting wit.

The grimness was only charming. Let the singular answer that Claude Rains gave to an interviewer on the macabre suffice for Gorey's: "I think playing villains is lovely! Often we'd like to do the very things we discipline ourselves against. Isn't it true?...In the movies I can be as mean, as wicked as I want to – and all without hurting anybody. 'Look at that lovely girl I've shot.'" Anything gruesome in the work of Edward Gorey comes across as funny and therefore innocent in the very same way that sexuality in the movies of Marilyn Monroe is made funny and innocent. A naïve and blatant, semi-serious but amusing irony flat-bottoms the excesses in both and renders them entirely harmless.

Gorey habitually used to drive at noon across town through Hyannis to Turner's for lunch – he could be hidebound – but when that restaurant closed, he drove (he didn't like to walk) down the street to Jack's Outback, a small lunch and breakfast nook in Yarmouthport where for lunch he invariably had potato salad with a slice of roast beef, an English muffin with cream cheese, fruit salad, and two Pepsi-Colas. He also liked hot dogs. For breakfast he ordered poached eggs, ham, and white toast. He usually sat alone in a booth, eating quietly with his nose in a paperback, unless one of the locals there plumped down beside him, as I often did, me and many another crashing bore in town who found Gorey so amusing that it was difficult to leave him to his onesies. A book in his hand could be anything. A few I do recall him reading were Llewelyn Powys's *The Verdict of Bridlegoose* which prompted him to ask, as I sat down, "Would you agree that sensuality is noisome?" And *Guide-Posts to Chinese Painting* by Louise Wallace Hackney, which intrigued him as it commemorates, among other

Paul Theroux, EG. Alexander Theroux, young Louis Theroux (ca. 1981).

things, the blade of grass as a model for the study of the straight line. Another was the interminable *Clarissa* ("in which an impenetrable woman is raped," said Gorey) of chubby Samuel Richardson – for some reason Gorey harbored a great love for the epistolary form and used it himself for several of his plays – denominated by my friend as "the greatest gasbag of all time." "I thought that the greatest gasbag of all time was Pindar," I said in reply. "Him, too." I particularly recall sitting there with Gorey one noon when he was discussing Stephen Leacock's ghost story, "Buggam Grange," James Baldwin's life-long anger, and, in an insuperably innocent way one would not have ascribed to him, the mysterious JFK assassin, "Saul," who supposedly was the villain who fired the fatal shots, all of the topics raised, by the way, in a linking rebus, as if in a logical context!

Gorey loved to eat, and I recall times when he appeared quite heavy. He liked my pot roast. He loved egg-nog, and scones. He had diabetes and had to avoid sweets, which was not easy for him. Fruitcake, I believe, was about the only food he truly disliked – and mocked. He liked to repeat that there were only a few fruitcakes in the world which, never eaten, were always being regifted around Christmas time. He habitually came and went. I know that once in a while he would head off with his cousins or friends to visit historic Highfield Hall in Falmouth, Mass. for occasional music programs, art exhibits, and culinary events. He also enjoyed visiting the great Whaling Museum in New Bedford. As I say, he was pretty much a man in the neighborhood. He never "jumped" for Philippe Halsman. He did not sit for Richard Avedon. He did not condescend to pinch his cheek for Annie Leibovitz.

The owner of Jack's Outback restaurant, the late Jack Braginton-Smith who was a notorious local curmudgeon – "You again?" he would bark at most customers who came in for lunch, his eyebrows raised like a flammulated owl – after having had his toe amputated (diabetes), was given the distinct honor of being the recipient of an original doggerel-poem by Edward Gorey. An original Gorey drawing stood by the cash register, where, when a person paid his or her check, Jack would loudly clang a bell. I would sit in the booth across from Gorey for an hour, delighted to talk to someone so opinionated and to be able to hear him fulminate with great exaggeration on the news of the day, the political mixed in with show business, a movie he had seen the previous night, some particular crotchet – "What kind of incandescent nonsense are we to swallow with that spot on television repeating over and over [derisive sing-song here] "Brown eggs are local eggs, and local eggs are fresh?" – the cost of a dump-sticker, or a national murder case. I remember he told me, narrating the dramatic, foible-ridden story with the precious hand-flaps he often employed when he recounted something wild, how he actually lost his mother's *ashes* in the house – she had been cremated, and the cremains were to be sent out to Ohio – but then, thank the Lord, managed to find them where they had originally been placed – in a paper bag! These all could have served as whimsical entries in his 1989 book, *The Dripping Faucet: Fourteen Hundred and Fifty-Eight Tiny, Tedious, & Terrible Tales,* a narrow foot-long "epic" of characters V and W, two anthropomorphized urns – some might insist that they are personified salt and pepper shakers – and their emotional ups and downs. I secretly suspect the book is a satire on the follies of marriage, or at least coupledom, the subject of a good deal of gay art.

Along with cats, Gorey loved tea; good paintings; iron rings; amateur theatricals; Celtic crosses, which he collected (he wore them around his neck); television; *Dick Van Dyke Show* reruns; ballet; the novels of Jane Austen; scarves; his Cuisinart; Keds sneakers (their fading from the American scene – Robert Frost also wore them, so did Rod McKuen – Gorey called a "disaster"); antique shows and flea markets; the *Golden Girls* TV sitcom; witty limericks; a glass of Glenfiddich, hard shaving soap, the palace purple coral bells of the perennial plant *Heuchera micrantha* – he also liked the papyrus, a monocot belonging to the sedge family – silent movies, and the actor James Cagney. He famously wore insect jewelry. You would see rings with scarabs on his fingers, a brass spider on a chain around his neck, bee pins, lizard brooches. (Have you ever heard of cremation jewelry? I remember discussing it with Gorey – talk about a subject dear to his heart – and had once even planned to give him for his birthday a "Tear of Love" sterling silver pendant-with-chain [18"] which can hold a small portion of a soul's cremated remains, a lock of hair, or dried ceremonial flowers, but at the time I could not scare up $69.95.) He loved the color taupe gray, but also odd off-colors such as moldy strawberry, mustard, and chutney. "Can you fathom anyone going out wearing hunter *orange*, never mind killing animals?" he once quite seriously asked me. He worshipped the choreographic visions of the late George Balanchine, whom he described for years as "the great living genius, in any of the arts." He also loved *The Rocky Horror Picture Show* and the novels of Patrick White. What made him like this or that is actually hard to say. But it had to be genuine, at least in its own terms. He loved TV's *Buffy the Vampire Slayer*, for example, and one of the main reasons he watched the show regularly was that he found it openly unpretentious and strictly camp. He would understand the idea, "She isn't a phony because she is a real phony," as Holly Golightly's agent in *Breakfast at Tiffany's* put it. It was unjustifiable ostentation he disliked. He greatly admired early animation, like Ferdinand Zecca's *The Egg Cracker Suite* and *Daffy the Dinosaur* and such stop-motion films from the 1920s as *Prehistoric Poultry, Morpheus Mike,* and *The Ghost of Slumber Mountain* by Willis O'Brien, the talented man who did the animation for *King Kong.* He was sure to watch any animation shows, claymation, full animation – Disney, etc. – rotoscoping, experimental, puppetoons, pixilation, 2-D, 3D, go motion, no motion, "anything except excruciatingly bad chipmunk movies," and I remember he even enjoyed the *Ren and Stimpy Show* which I believe had something of a reputation for indecent humor. "'Teeth to the left of me! Gums to the right of me! I tell you I can't stand it! I'm going mad!'" he used to quote, whatever that meant. I believe many animators sought Gorey out.

He devised marionettes and hand puppets: Figbash, his own odd bird-headed creation that first appeared in *The Raging Tide; or The Black Doll's Imbroglio* (1987) and then began popping up as a figure in his plays, on posters, and as a beanbag more or less became Gorey's icon. Tiny home-made bean bags stuffed with rice that he idly sewed featuring that creature, along with bats, cats, dragons, hippos etc., now considered original Gorey art, are selling for as much as $500 a pop. A large lobster claw that he stood up – he referred to it as the "*foetus perdu*"– who can say, might one day fall into the category of creative kitsch, right up there with a Joseph Cornell box or a Jasper Johns's sculptured paint can or a Kurt Schwitters wheel (that turned only to the right, satirizing Nazi Germany) or Marcel Duchamp's avant-garde *Fountain,* signed R. Mutt! As I said, he breathed to read. He liked poetry. He told me that in college he had memorized almost all the poems – the entire canon – of W. H. Auden. He also loved cinnamon toast; soap operas; *Leave It to June* ("my favorite musical," he once told me, a movie I have to confess I had never heard of and to which to this day I have never found a single reference); famous criminal cases; and bad behavior, fictional and real. He said, "I'm a great aficionado – that's the word everybody uses – of true crime."

"Crime tells us in detail about the way people really live," declared Gorey, who was completely convincing on the subject, at least to me, citing the revelations, instructive if insidious, of secret lives, of anti-social behavior,

EG directing his play, *The Raging Tide.*

of cruelty and brutish wrath. Needless to say, he was word-perfect on the various plots and turns of the world's famous cases and such well-known crimes such as the infamous Lizzie Borden Case of 1892, which fascinated him. I often tried to convince Gorey that the [ice!] ax-murderer of Andrew and Abby Borden was in fact the Jewish ice-cream peddler Hyman Lubinsky [1868-1928], aged 24 in 1892 – I even wrote a poem about it – who claimed to have seen a strange woman crossing from the Borden barn to the side door on the fateful day of the murders. Lubinsky and Lizzie I think had something going for some time. He knew by sight the Borden maid, Bridget Sullivan, and swore this woman was not Bridget. Lizzie of course claimed to have been out in the barn up in the hayloft for some time doing various things when someone must have murdered her father in the sitting room. Lizzie claimed to have come inside after hearing a noise, putting her hat down, then discovering Mr. Borden dead on the sofa. Lubinsky whose grasp of the English language was poor, was somewhat muddled on the stand – intentionally? – changing his times and offering fumbled explanations. Naturally the defense for Lizzie was delighted to make the most of Lubinsky's tale as it seemed to back up Lizzie's own version of events and supported the story she had been in the barn. Lubinsky, however never said the woman he saw in the very narrow alley between the Churchill house and the Borden side door was wearing any hat. I drove out to take a photo of the Lubinsky monument (the legend is all in Hebrew) in the Hebrew Cemetery in Fall River and gave it to Gorey as a birthday present on February 22, 1982. But it was not merely that case alone that intrigued Gorey. They all did. The Black Dahlia. The Tichbourne Affair. The Profumo case. Charles Starkweather. The Boston Strangler. The Christie murders. Thelma Todd. And of course the Yorkshire Ripper saga. No murder case went unignored. "I've seen every mad-slasher movie ever made," he told me.

Mystery moves a Gorey story. He loved provocation. To what end? Just to make you think. There are red herrings to be found throughout his fables – an enigmatic note, a piece of paper, writing on an urn, eerie sounds from the far wing of an estate, a chance figure lurking in the shrubbery. "It doesn't mean anything" was one of Gorey's standard remarks whenever he was asked a question – questions for which he had small patience, by the way – about some apparent clue or other in one of his stories. *QRV*, enigmatic initials never explained and also the title of one of his small books, is a "universal solvent," which figures elusively in several of his plays. When asked about it, Gorey's answer was exactly what Homer Simpson said about beer: "It is the cause of and solution to all life's problems." *The Awdrey-Gore Legacy* (1972) – a book that compiles a sparingly-narrated collection of evidence, jottings, and suppositions compiled by the investigator (who has a penchant for quoting the *Ipsiad*) – is Gorey's contribution to the world of Raymond Chandler, Dashiell Hammett, and James M. Cain. The crime is laid out: on last St. Spasmus's day Miss D. Awdrey-Gore was found dead at the age of 97. Just before dawn a nameless poacher came upon her body in a disused fountain on the estate of Lord Ravelflap; she was seated bolt upright on a gilt ballroom chair, one of a set of seventeen then on display at Suthick & Upter's Auction Rooms in Market Footling; her left hand clutching a painted tin lily of cottage manufacture, inside which was rolled up a Cad's Relish label of a design superseded in 1947; something illegible was pencilled on the back. That she had been murdered was obvious, though as yet the cause of death has not been determined. One intriguing page in the book is a smattering of notes on the case written carefully on specially-prepared note cards, salient matter that one has to address as a detective would in order to solve the crime. To wit:

> *What the murderer failed to realize is that there is no Number Fourteen, Bandage Terrace*
> *Lesla Trope is really Lord Onion's great grand-daughter*
> *What the murderer failed to realize is that yellow stitchbane is not yellow at all, but a pale mauve*
> *At 4:17 the door to the winter garden was already locked and bolted*
> *James Grumesdaub and Charles Toast are really the same person.*
> *What the murderer failed to realize is that the Great Northwest Road does not go beyond Little Remorse*
> *George Utmost is really not Daphne Sost's cousin from Wyoming*
> *On the 14th of January the "Larko Sandargo" was still off the coast of Iceland*
> *What the murderer failed to realize is that Grumblotch's salts are not soluble in lemonade*
> *Lady Truss is really two entirely different people*
> *What the murderer failed to realize is that at high tide the outermost of Saint Loola's Rocks is completely submerged*

I have referred to W.H. Auden. The poet was roughly a quarter century older than Gorey. The two had a lot in common, however, and many comparisons could be made with the two, for both shared many similarities, including birthdays, almost – Auden was born on February 21, Gorey the next day. I do think that in the light of Gorey's mad admiration for Auden, knocking the two together might be profitable to some degree. "Auden was by nature solitary; few people ever knew him well," we read in *Auden in Love* written by Dorothy J. Farnan, a longtime member of the Auden-Kallmann circle. (She was married to Kallmann's father.) "He kept hidden from the world the ultimate secret of his nature and thus tended to inspire awe even in his most intimate friends – all, that is, except Chester [Kallmann, his partner]. I wonder if Gorey in his admiration for him did not take a page out of Auden's personality. Both collected books with a passion and had piles of them – smoke-stacks! – in their apartments and both loved to read detective stories. Both lived for decades in New York City, Auden in Brooklyn Heights, Gorey in the Murray Hill District. Both loved good food (Chester Kallmann was a gourmet chef). Gorey drank little alcohol, whereas Auden drank Smirnoff, martinis, red wine, and cognac, although he shunned pot and confessed to having, under a doctor's supervision, tried LSD. "Nothing much happened, but I did get the distinct impression that some birds were trying to communicate with me." Neither of the two ever taught, although Auden did occasionally lecture. Curiously both did stints in the Army, Auden in the U.S. Strategic Bombing Survey. (He came to the States in 1939, when he more or less put political ideas away.) He felt guilty – "All that we are not stares back at what we are," he once wrote – and was no more than Gorey a student of soldiery. "Bombing does no good," Auden declared at one point. "But you know how army people are. They don't like to hear things that run contrary to what they've thought." Humbug and pretense in the extreme could drive both of them batty.

Both were men of generally fixed and inflexible habits. Auden got up at six a.m., always wore slippers, hated sunshine, never worked after three p.m. – which as the result of a somewhat belated insight he aligned to that being the canonical hour of Christ's crucifixion – and, as I say, imbibed a good deal, far more than Gorey who drank very little. Auden always had a vermouth before lunch, with lunch a beer, and as he said "at ten to six I start on vodka martinis, at dinner I have wine." He never wrote when he was drunk. Auden, who was not at all averse to the low-brow or to kitsch, often sported a Tolkien

EG's *Flapping Ankles* was first performed in 1991.

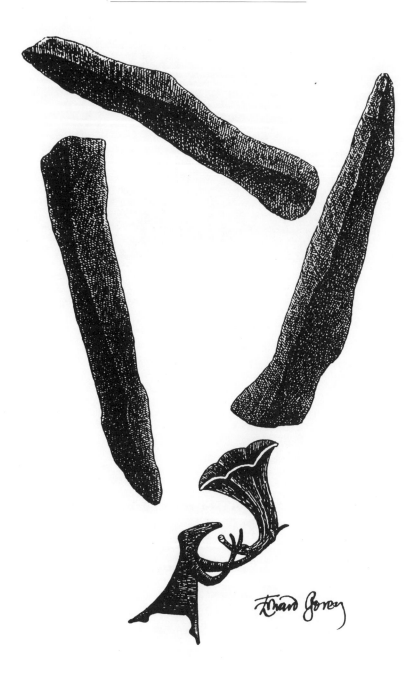

A program drawing for EG's play, *QRV.*

sweater, which he loved, adored musicals ("*Kiss Me, Kate* is more fun than *The Taming of the Shrew*," he declared), and wrote not only indecent poems as well as cheeky limericks, a popular one of which went as follows –

> *The Bishop elect of Hong Kong*
> *Had a dong that was twelve inches long.*
> *He thought the spectators*
> *Were admiring his gaiters*
> *When he went to the gents'. He was wrong.*

– but also pornography, in fact. A poem that Auden composed in 1948, "The Platonic Blow," 34 stanzas (a-b-a-b), circulated in typescript for years and even saw print, pirated, in a small New York magazine called *Fuck You: a magazine of the arts* which in the end, Auden complained, did not even have the grace to pay him. There were other marked differences between the two. Auden, unlike Gorey, went to church on Sundays and believed in the devil and even had somewhat to do with shaping the beauty of the Psalms. Auden was less eccentric. There were no fur coats or multiple rings or lobster-walking: the poses that he struck were all intellectual. What wowed his contemporaries was the way he said things, especially when he wrote them down. Auden grew crankier in his later years; Gorey controlled himself when he was nettled and in such instances always withdrew. No sharper distinction between the two could be made than in their preferred modes of entertainment. Gorey we know loved movies. "All movies, except the comic – Charlie Chaplin and the Marx Brothers were quite funny – and rock and roll are all taboo," pronounced W. H. Auden. (Gorey however dismissed the Marx Brothers as hectic immature pranksters, amusing only to silly people, and I agree with him.) At a dinner party with Stravinsky in Berlin, as reported by Robert Craft, Auden unequivocally stated that "any claim for the cinema as an art is rubbish." Almost in the same breath he also said, "I also want to do a poem explaining why photography is not an art." Auden was far more impatient than Gorey. ("I'm terribly short-tempered.") He equally loathed the whole idea of television. "Personally, I don't see how any civilized person can watch TV, far less own a set," said Auden. "I prefer detective stories, especially Father Brown." A homosexual who thought homosexuality wicked, Auden believed that as a gay man one was acting out either the mother-son relationship (oral) or the man-woman relationship (anal). It would be as far-fetched to hear

Edward Gorey say such things as it would be to find a Trappist monk banging a bass-drum.

It may be pointed out here that, although Auden preferred highbrow queens and smart or precocious college guys, the most beautiful lyric that he ever composed was written to a teenage boy, "Lay your sleeping head, my love, / Human on my faithless arm; / Time and fevers burn away / Individual beauty from / Thoughtful children…" He also slept with women, one back in 1945 named Rhoda Jaffe, a comely, divorced Jewish woman who not only did secretarial work for him, mostly typing his manuscripts, but was his lover. It is said gay marriages are between lovers, and as Marina Tsvetaeva put it in her touching little handbook for lesbians, *Mon frère féminin,* lovers are children and children do not have children. Auden seems never to have slept with Kallmann after an early traitorous affair. Nevertheless he seems to have obtained from their long alliance together a certain amount of peace and quiet.

Auden, like our friend, loved cats. Both had a number of them and went to great trouble naming them. Living with Auden and Chester Kallman were the felines Lucina, the Duchess, Nero, Dorabella, Rudimac, of course, of whom Auden once notably wrote, "Cats can be very funny, and have the oddest ways of showing they're glad to see you. Rudimac always peed in our shoes." He even had a dog, Mosé, whom Auden found shivering in a swamp. In his New York apartment was their calico cat, Cenerentola (It. for Cinderella), named for the opera by Gioachino Rossini, *La Cenerentola, ossia La bontà in trionfo* (*Cinderella, or Goodness Triumphant*). Auden and Chester, according to Farnan, habitually referred to their cats in conversation. "Lucina is such a snob, my dear – She won't even talk to Nero," "Nero simply adores eels and ate one alive for breakfast," etc. It was only after some time passed that a newcomer to the conversation was able to discover that Wystan and Chester were talking about cats. When you visited him, Edward Gorey was always filling you in on what his cats did or were doing. "Look, Agrippina thinks she is Maria Plisetskaya doing a *grand battement en cloche*," he would say. "Kanzuke, like rhubarb, hates wet feet." "Kokiden is well past his sell-by date this morning, judging by that furiously untidy fur," "I suspect Murasake is a Burkeian. He believes neither in permanent victories nor in permanent defeats. But he does believe in permanent values." Did Gorey just think these things up on the spot? Oh, it was all very heady. Neither Gorey nor Auden went so far as the Italian writer Elsa Morante, who believed that animals are angels and claimed that one of her cats, Guiseppe, was "the other half of her soul. Morante once actually wrote a calligram to the film director Pier Paolo Pasolini in the shape of a cat (*madrigale in forma di gatto*).

W.H. Auden, Swinburne, Hart Crane, like Gorey, all loved cats and wrote about them. Edmund Gosse, who kept cats throughout his life – Atossa, his favorite, was a gift from the ornate professor Walter Pater – used to amuse his guests by nursing a cat swathed in a napkin. It may be a gay thing to revere them to excess. I don't know. Henry James once beat a cat to death for some reason, I remember reading with some shock. It was after all James who once declared, "Cats and monkeys; monkeys and cats; all human life is there."

Auden, like Gorey, offered strong opinions, expressing them without effort or pretense, and had not only a penchant for droll, intelligent, gossipy conversation but outlandish, comic *pronunciamenti*. "Rilke was the greatest Lesbian poet since Sappho," Auden once stated. "Yevtushenko wrote the poor man's *Howl*." Discussing homosexuality, he insisted "Shakespeare was in the homintern." And to an English critic in Berlin who was defending Debussy's *Pelléas et Mélisande*, "No, dear, you take it from mother, *Pelléas* is shit." Neither had any illusions about human nature, nor regarded mankind sentimentally. Sublime was not their estimate of man. They despised humbug and pretense. I suspect in some regard they were always on commando duty, obliged to pronounce about one thing, or another with talk invariably tending to come in at a slant, almost always tricked out with irony. A methodic androgyny managed to hold sway with both. To put it one way, candytuft grew next to cucumber. A snippet from an Auden letter of January 18, 1949 could have been written by Gorey:

> *Heard a wonderful performance of Figaro with Sayão, Steber, Tajo, Busch; an equally wonderful* Barbiere, *with Valdengo, who is a great singer; and a horrendous* Walküre. *Max Lorenz as Siegmund was inaudible. The Cowbell's gown was pure Westchester, and Stiedry, my dear, doesn't know his baton from his bum.*

"The Cowbell" was a name that Chester gave to Helen Traubel, a famous Wagnerian soprano of the 1940s and 1950s whose singing he could not abide. It was typical of the kind of verbal wit and gentle mockery we associate with the two.

EG's *QRV* was first performed in 1990.

As we have seen, in any conversation, Gorey's random, off-hand banter and general *mode de parlance* was always arch. He was given to gnomic or dogmatic remarks, the way Dr. Samuel Johnson was, and of course knew that they were entertaining, Auden knew the mode, of course, the persona of the orator who must say unique things in public, and many of his remarks were hilarious and quotable: "Chianti tastes like red ink," "Writing nasty reviews can be fun," "No woman is an aesthete," "The idea of debt appalls me," "No gentleman can fail to admire Bellini," "I don't think good work ever makes one cry," "The problem with behaviourists is that they always manage to exclude themselves from their theories," "As great as Dante might have been, I wouldn't have had the slightest wish to have known him personally. He was a terrible prima donna."

Gorey would sardonically but almost always with a bright laugh refer to certain people with an epithet that he felt applied. "Teresa Toscanini and his glowering baton" was one I remember. It is a typically gay thing, using alliterative camp names, such as "Gertie Graves," Auden's particular name for the poet Robert Graves, or "Enervating Edna" – Auden despised Edna St. Vincent Millay. On the subject of love, neither of them seemed to have faith in the state, or at least any conviction in the emotion that it seemed tenable. I had always concluded ever since I met Ted that, regarding the matter of love, his attitude was quite straightforward: plain and simply, he felt well out of it. I suspect he felt love consumed one, and, worse, often turned into hate, that it was rarely joyful, peaceful or comforting. Whenever I would happen to visit Gorey after some horrible *contretemps* or other with whatever girlfriend I had at the time, I could never help but gauge my own frazzled or unbandaged condition with his comparatively serene self-reassurance, the almost chaste state of singlehood about him, an almost ethical essence, a kind of blessedness. No one having reined him in imparted to Gorey an aura of liberty and laughing insouciance that so many seemed to lack. He appeared to be blithely free, in every sense. In this way, he seemed to achieve, to realize, all of his dreams. He despised authority. That alone is a libertarian trope, if not to be envied then at least to be saluted.

Early in their relationship, Auden caught his partner, Chester, in a flagrant infidelity and would never forget it. This violation of faith was a profound shock to Auden – he had worn a wedding ring to indicate his understanding of the relationship – and he went so far as to contemplate actually murdering Kallman's lover. The two lived together again, until the end, but without passion. "What I think ruins so many marriages is this romantic idea of falling in love," Auden told the *Paris Review*.

> *It happens, of course, I suppose to some people who are possessed of unusually fertile imaginations. Undoubtedly it is a mystical experience which occurs. But with most people who think they are in love I think the situation can be described far more simply, and, I'm afraid, brutally. The trouble with all this love business is one or the other partner ends up feeling bad or guilty because they don't have it the way they've read it. I'm afraid things went off a lot more happily when marriages were arranged by parents... And, with Goethe, I think marriages should be celebrated more quietly and humbly, because they are the beginning of something. Loud celebrations should be saved for successful conclusions.*

Gorey was very private about strictly personal matters, as why wouldn't he be, and although sardonic a gentle. caring fellow, very neat, who never quite caught up to his pile of work he'd promised. He quit smoking in the early 1970s. Auden smoked – "Everything he touched turns to cigarettes," said Louis MacNeice – bit his fingernails, was obsessively punctual, sartorially sloppy, was more open, and capable of being grumpy. He disliked sweets.

Not so Gorey. He loved Oreo cookies with a passion. He loved to receive Christmas presents. He liked shopping at the British Book Centre on 55th St. in Manhattan. He was fond of Ian Fleming and the Bond books *long before* they became popular in the United States, and I believe joined in the peculiar if harmless habit Bond fanatics have in always sending cards to each other signed "007." I have mentioned Turner's, until it closed one of his favorite luncheon spots; he craved two desserts there, one, their coffee brandy ice-cream with Java sauce on top and, two, their raspberry mousse. But he wasn't fussy. He enjoyed – relied on is perhaps the better way to put it – TV dinners and kept a stack of them in his refrigerator, where there were also a good many cans of chocolate syrup. "He loved my eggnog muffins and grape-nut custard," one of his very good friends, former fashion-illustrator Evelyn Ramalhete, once proudly told me. "I miss Ted so much, every day. After he passed away, I took

Alice, his little Calico cat." She paused and softly said, "I have the Tony Award he won for *Dracula*." Perhaps more than anything else, Gorey loved statement. He painted his toenails black on the day Gertrude Stein died, then forgot about it, went to the beach and surprised himself with his ardor.

He was peaceful and for almost lava-lamp comfort kept in several rooms at home bowls of fat green marbles covered with water. That's right. They just sat there on table or desks, like water boscages evoking, at least to me, a very Asian mood. Bookshelves and old trestle tables – beautiful old woods – predominated in his Yarmouthport house. The house had hardwood floors, hooked rugs, antique chairs and tables. There were long rows of videocassettes in his upstairs rooms. All of Mozart on LPs, CDs. A television set sprouting all kinds of boxes and wands and remotes. His kitchen, in which whenever I stopped by we always sat talking, having tea – Lapsang Souchong, which gives off the scent of freshly-tarred roads at fifty yards – and white toast sprinkled with cinnamon, was quiet and cool.

Do you know something else that Gorey loved? Gorey positively loved names. Hiccupboro. Willowdale. Iron Hills. Just the names of places. The Vinegar Works. The Clogsock Yacht Club. Williboo Lake. Doubtful Footings. Vignettes in his play, *Lost Shoelaces*, performed in 1987 by Magical Oyster Theater at Woods Hole, had titles like "The Yellow Thingummy," "The Back Ladder Variations," and "The Creaking Knot," among others. In *The Blue Aspic* (1968), "my opera book," the diva Ortenzia Caviglia (it means "ankle" in Italian) has as her manager a chap called Abrogio Rigaglie. Ambrose Giblets. Maudie Splaytoe. Mrs. Ümlaut. Octavia Prong. La Dame aux Pample-Mousses. M. Bandage-Herniaire. The Comtesse de Macache Bezef. Other characters elsewhere are named Purgatory, Waffle, and Kachoo. "Figbash threw an antimacassar over Skrump" goes a line from *The Raging Tide* (1987). Over the years Gorey and I found mirthful the names of many of the characters that have appeared in various Henry James stories, names like Fleda Vetch, Weeks Wimbush, Mildred Theory, Gwendolyn Ambient, Bessie Mangler, Amy Frush, Rosanna Gaw, and Lady Augusta Minch. There is even a furnished apartment in a James story, *In The Cage*, that is named Thrupp! (Gorey was convinced, incidentally, that the name Meryl Streep was actually a Jamesian invention!) But why go further than some of the typical titles of Gorey's own summer puppet plays? *Lost Shoelaces, Tinned Lettuce, Chinese Gossip, Flapping Ankles, Crazed Teacups. English Soup,* a series of rapid-fire skits which he staged at the Cotuit Center for the Arts in 1998, he later took to

Hollywood, where I am told it had a great success. And how well I remember the loud mutt-laugh I had when first opening his wonderful "novel," *The Unstrung Harp,* and read with great delight,

Mr. Earbrass has driven over to Nether Millstone in search of forced greengages, but has been distracted by a bookseller's.

Rummaging among mostly religious tracts and privately printed reminiscences, he has come across The Meaning of the House, *his second novel. In making sure it has not got there by mistake (as he would hardly care to pay more for it), he discovers it's a presentation copy.* For Angus – will you ever forget the bloaters? *Bloaters? Angus?*

If he loved words, it goes without saying that he liked sentences. No one has written funnier, more intriguing, more brocaded lines: "Last night it did not seem as if today it would be raining." "In the blue horror of dawn the vines in the carpet appear likely to begin twining up his ankles." "Over the Carmargue a great dark bird flew into the propeller of the aeroplane." "They sat down to a meal of cornflakes and treacle, turnip sandwiches, and artificial grape soda." "I want to say knockwurst," another fellow suddenly exclaims out of the blue.

Gorey also had lots of peeves. He hated brussels sprouts, false sentiment, minimal art, overcommitment to work, being solicited for blurbs, the music of Andrew Lloyd Webber, the works of the Marquis de Sade ("absolutely paralyzing prose"), churchgoing, Nixon and Agnew, right-wingers, discussions about his own work, prattling and didactic fools, and *all* Al Pacino movies. He referred to Pacino in one of his *Soho* reviews as "the name of a local hole in space." I remember a long time ago going into Hyannis with him to see the turkey, *Bobby Deerfield* (1977), and Gorey literally moaned through the entire movie, squawking, "Oh for the Christ's sake!" and snapping several times out loud, "Can someone please tell me what this is in *aid* of?" We stayed to the end, barely. "There are only two reasons I'll walk out of a movie," he once told me. "One, if an animal is being abused, shot, killed or hurt in any way. Oh please! And two, *any* birth scenes! I spent entire segments in the foyer during *Hawaii* with Julie Andrews heavy with pheasant and howling in hospital stirrups, and to this day I wonder why I did not continue all the way home!" At the very beginning of the film, *The Left Hand of God,* while crossing a bridge in a brutal storm that capsizes him into a raging river, Humphrey Bogart,

Straying author from *The Unstrung Harp*.

EG's Crazed Teacups was first performed in 1992.

playing a priest, manages to crawl onto land but never looks back as the small donkey he is riding simultaneously goes plunging miserably under the terrible torrents of water. Gorey – he repeated this to me several times – half-angry, half-depressed – told me that he "harrumphed" out of the theater. He could say with the Vachel Lindsay of "The Santa Fe Trail" in *Congo and Other Poems,*

> *I want live things in their pride to remain.*
> *I will not kill one grasshopper vain,*
> *Though he eats a hole in my shirt like a door.*
> *I let him out, give him one chance more.*
> *Perhaps, while he gnaws my hat in his whim,*
> *Grasshopper lyrics occur to him.*

It may be pointed out that his choice to wear fur coats preceded his love of animals, or let us say he would not let his position on animal exploitation become the occasion of thwarting his way of life. He jettisoned wearing raccoon fur coats later in life, eventually feeling guilty for having worn them. Most of those big fur coats Gorey wore for the decades he lived in New York City – raccoon, beaver, sable, mink, and wolf, he wore them all – were actually women's coats that he had purchased over the years at thrift shops, according to his good friend, John Heaney, who explained to me that he was "quite a sight walking down Fifth avenue, completely oblivious to any comments or stare," looking as "notable," as novelist D. Keith Mano memorably put it, "as Truman Capote on the Boston Bruins' bench." One has no problem somehow imagining the gawkers, *bouche béante,* watching him pass.

They say appearances are deception, but deception is half the battle for that kind of man determined to explore dimensions and not be beaten into the same kind of dull, flat, craven, unadventurous servitude the world offers. It may not always be attractive. Have you noticed, for example, how men often sadly typify the very things they attack? Conformity, nevertheless, kills. As Aldous Huxley once remarked, "Trees in the mass can be almost terrible."

There are other things Gorey could not stand: television evangelists and their shameless simony, the novels of Judith Krantz, extreme feminism ("*Women poets?* Who needs this kind of anthology?"), travel, women reporters who always cover stories looking through the "as a mom myself" prism, invitations with the, to him, inconsiderate R.S.V.P. that omitted the proviso, "If you are able to be present." He thought the Reverend Jesse Jackson a complete phony and Bill Cosby an oaf and classic hypocrite who wrote a book called *Fatherhood* and then proceeded to pay $100,000 over 20 years not only to keep an extramarital affair with his mistress Shawn Upshaw a secret but their illegitimate daughter, Autumn Jackson, because she threatened to go public about him. Right-wing pea-and-thimble men and so-called "broadcasters" such as the grouping of tendentious and fraudulent people like Paul Harvey, Rush Limbaugh, and G. Gordon Liddy could make him positively apoplectic. As I say, Nixon for his pusillanimity, his paltriness, his almost diabolical shape-shifting, and his swinish deceit represented virtually everything Gorey loathed – sulfur and nitrate – whenever the two came together, even in the abstract of topical conversation, it went boom! I once heard him compare the one-time Republican vice-president and felon, Spiro Agnew, to a "vulcanized India-rubber ball." He hated curtains on windows and rugs in a room. He loved mysteries, but only good ones, drawing a sharp line at the kind of fat, over-larded best-sellers Stephen King turned out by the pound, dismissing them with a groan as a "farrago of endless, inauthentic prose undermining the already receding levels of reality." The articles in *The New York Review of Books* he repeatedly denounced as being "more long-winded than Nestor's grandfather." Kitsch amused him only in *small* objects.

He abhorred flattery. Flattery is by definition insincere. I recall a time a decade or so ago when the PBS network in Boston, WGBH sent down a crew to Cape Cod to film an interview with him. An acquaintance of mine there asked me what to avoid by way of chit-chat, and I said, "Flattery." The predictable result of course was that the interviewer proceeded immediately to ignore my advice and in the most ham-handed way to dump a truckload of blandishments on Gorey's head. An agitated Gorey sealed up like a clam. Fakery, bluffing, in its every phase nettled him. I believe that over a lifetime he had been served up a lot of such jelly omelets. It was all of it meaninglessness, "moon-faced Nonsense, that erudite forger," in the words of his beloved W. H. Auden. "I see," he would reply with a cold monotone to all excessive and insincere effusions directed at him, and the two words always – *always* – had an audible frost on them to anyone with a discerning ear. Violence did not shock him. He found pornography tiresome. ("So dull. There are just so many places where one can stick things. The Marquis de Sade was just a mechanical reversal of all the ordinary moralities. And to read the stuff! He's one of the world's worst writers.")

Gorey was allergic to wool. He refused to answer his telephone after six o'clock at night. He told me more than once that he never really liked New York City; even when living there, he spent more than half his time on Cape Cod. He was sour and cynical about glory and galas and gatherings ("Usually my work is exhibited as part of a cookie festival with tennis," he would say.) "I hate movies about *ea*-ting," he would singsong with a malicious lilt, "like *My Dinner With André* and *Like Water For Chocolate*." We used to laugh about Mormon names like Orvil, Aaronica, Clebert, Uri, and Enoch. He disliked the Ulster accent, talk radio, marzipan, CD cellophane that is impossible to open, the trashy interviews of Barbara Walters, and especially zoos. He disliked anyone in a rage and anything in a cage. He thought Israel was too bullyingly aggressive and over-reaching. He disliked Republicans. He once told me, "A lot of pre-Columbian art is too cute." Although he collected so many different and diverse things – might this not be an example of what physicist Niels Bohr referred to as complimentarity? – Gorey disliked avarice. "What is the worst of all human vices ?" he was once asked. His immediate response was, "Greed." Smarmy hustlers of first-editions and avaricious second-hand booksellers who asked him to sign books and then went on to peddle them particularly irked him. "We are...double in ourselves, so that we believe what we disbelieve and cannot rid ourselves of what we condemn," insightfully wrote Montaigne, and if I am not mistaken I have to say I believe Gorey, for his wide reach, in spite of his love of objects, was in that unequivocal reply regarding greed not excluding himself from that particular excess of human folly.

I was pleased in one of my last chats with him to convince him with a battery of good arguments how perfectly stupid the overrated Chaplin film *The Great Dictator* is, with its strutting grammar-school humor and impossible silliness. On the other hand, he gently mocked me for once confessing to him that I can never watch the last wistful ten minutes of Gregory Peck and Audrey Hepburn in *Roman Holiday* without tears in my eyes. He was not a particularly enthusiastic admirer of the medical profession. He disliked doctors and hated hospitals and didn't "do" wakes. He had a known bad heart condition. He would speak jokingly about his "enfeebled condition." He had diabetes and suffered from insomnia in his last year and took the time, uncharacteristically, to see a psychotherapist about it. "Do I look demented?" he asked a friend at lunch with a smirk after one such

EG's *English Soup* was first performed in 1998.

session. He had noticeably lost weight and looked quite pale. Tragically, only six days before the day he suffered what proved to be his untimely fatal heart attack, a Wednesday, he had been told by his physician to check in to Hyannis hospital for five days' observation, but he refused to do so. It was his particular way of dealing with things that he ignored what he disliked. It was his way with questions, when someone, say, tried to introduce a note of sobriety about some disaster. His contortions of self-reflection, a craning neck looking west into the middle-distance to deliberate, to deflect seriousness, almost always gave rise to a subversive quip and a stab at galgenhumor.

Gorey's sense of humor was arch, ironic, subversive, uncommon, informed, barbed, and highly allusive, nothing like all those hopelessly unfunny contemporary dorks we have long had to put up with like Art Buchwald, P.J. O'Rourke, Dave Barry, David Sedaris – the Art Linkletters of humor –nothing like the almost deafeningly bad TV crap of workaday buffoons like Jimmy Kimmel or Bill Maher or any of those dirty or flatulent Jewish comedians like Joan Rivers, Bob Saget, Lenny Bruce, and Alan King, all full of that stale old humor of the 1960s of the Jack Douglas-sort who wrote those books of side-splitting humor with splendiferous titles like *Shut Up and Eat Your Snowshoes* and *Never Trust A Naked Bus Driver.* His was never gag stuff, nothing like 1950s' wackery like Rootie Kazootie, Foodini and Pinhead, Judy Splinters, or Stan Freberg or witless Red Skelton or awful Bob Hope. What amused Gorey always had a touch of a *distress* element in it. His wit was caustic, his humor snarky, upending, in the tradition of people like Paul Lynde, Nathan Lane, Robert Morse, and scarifying British comic actors like Kenneth Williams, Derek Nimmo, and Clement Freud, the exaggerated punsters and literate quipsters of the BBC Radio 4 comedy panel game "Just A Minute." An original like Gorey – are you surprised? – had a colossally original mind, shaped like no other. He did not play to or give in to the work-a-day. He kept his humor, like his powder, dry. He was committed but cautious. Although it is clear that he did go to certain extremes whenever caught up in the grip of a new or sudden passion – a catalogue item he had to have, say, a book he had to read, a looming must-see film (and possibly see over and over) – he was certainly not a "100 Percenter"-type in Richard Hofstadter's sense of the term, going overboard with fanatical enthusiasm, madly spin-fitting. He was far too skeptical, too cautious, too detached, and too selective to do so.

I once asked him about tiresome and one-gets-the-very-distinct-impression-not-very-intelligent Martha Stewart, the Queen of Whitebread Living, a humorless and autocratic drone full of self-regard who desperately tries to come off a real queen but with all her "helpful hints" and dogged handiwork is actually the ultimate *maid* – she even bears the first name of the well-known Biblical potwalloper – whereupon Gorey groaned loudly and cried, "Get me a big mallet!" Other notable mallet candidates for him from the entertainment world, were, as I say, the preposterous Kathie Lee Gifford ("her facial contortions would be excessive on Daffy Duck"); speech-challenged self-promoter Barbara Walters; the "idiot" Maya Angelou who always pedantically insists that she be introduced at public events as "Maya Angel*o*" but then in her books makes about fifteen grammatical howlers per page; and of course the shameless Lauren Bacall, a former Hollywood beauty who is currently doing catfood commercials in which, apparently immune to irony, she farcically croons, "Good taste is *eaaaaasy* to recognize." When I once told Gorey that that vulgar, self-appointed interviewing buck-and-wing couple, overweening Joan Rivers and her daughter, Melissa, with that pulled-snout of theirs and those slit-sneaky and sidelong, mistrustful eyes looked to me exactly like hungry and angry timber wolves, he replied, "And they actually *paw* people!"

Gorey insisted that Woody Allen was a complete fraud, and he could not stand actress Meryl Streep. "Oh please!" said he, "every time she opens her mouth, the critics insist *Dostoevsky's* speaking!" He paused. "And who's even dippier is Glenn Close. Sexless as a teabag. Neither man, not woman, nor in-between! Julia Roberts's face looks like it's made of rubber – remember those Snap, Crackle, and Pop cartoon faces? And of course Streisand, God help us, I won't even go to see." Gorey loathed her with a passion, even more than John Waters does. I once heard him fulminate for a good half-hour on the impossible stupidity of her 1962 hit, "People," a song that, with its mawkish, politically correct soul-sharing, shriekingly embodies to a T everything that Edward Gorey utterly loathed:

"Pee-pull, pee-pull who need pee-pull are the luuu-kiest pee-pull in the wooooorld!"

I cannot honestly think of a single sentiment that would have driven Edward Gorey battier faster than the flaccid lyrics of that song with its, to him, canasta-closeness, hideous interconnect-edness, and ultimate meaninglessness.

He was not particularly keen on "human moments." Not for him to be quoting from Psalm 133 ("Behold how good and how pleasant it is for brethren to dwell together in unity.") or give public recitations of Ecclesiastes 4:9-11 ("Two are better than one because they have a good reward for their labor, for if they fall, the one will lift up his fellow and woe to him who is alone when he falls and has not another to lift him up. Again, if two lie together, then they have warmth; but how can one be warm alone?"). I know he loved W.C. Fields, and, although in a much more light-hearted way, they shared a like curmudgeonliness, a persona to which both seemed to devote, belying it somewhat, a positive energy. He was not a Mummer or Mason and knew not the answer to the question, "Is There No Help For The Widow's Son?" nor was he a Mormon who yearned to peep through either the Urim or the Thummim. As to joining the Elks, the Moose, the Rotary, the Gloatery, the Beavers or the Cleavers, I don't think so. Connectedness he fully preferred to leave to Amtrak couplings.

George Bernard Shaw said he went to church for recreation. "I like the solitariness," he insisted and often repeated the story of how when Queen Victoria was eighteen, they came to her and, explaining she was Queen of England, advised her of her office. The young girl asked whether she could really do what she liked, and, when this was reluctantly admitted by her careful mother, Victoria considered what wonderful and hitherto impossible happiness she could confer on herself by her new powers. And she could think of nothing more delightful than an hour of separate solitary confinement. It is not something many understand today, when technology has cut badly into the meditative.

I say Gorey was outside the whole circle. He liked being in the minority. Eccentrics in the United States, unlike in England, are often seen as threats. We tend to fear and ostracize such creatures. They are marginals, not democratic, to be feared – *different*. I'm afraid no trait is more winning in this country than conformity. Nixon, Bush, Reagan – just to pick some Republicans – were all middle-of-the-road boors. The Kennedys, ludicrously raised to royal-like heights over the years by craven hero-worshippers, were, are, surely among the most conventional families in the country. That is only politicians. To explain Oprah Winfrey's huge popularity on television I would cite nothing more than her pure conventionalism: *she always takes the side of the audience*, she is the Queen of Ordinariness.

An early photo of EG swimming (ca. 1950).

Among friends, the illustrator Edward Gorey was known for being a man who wished to live "deliberately," in the way of Henry David Thoreau. I have to say I considered him a mentor, however odd and reclusive a one he was, precisely on that score, for, Emerson was right, "discontent is the want of self-reliance," and no one was more self-reliant or content as he walked about this world than Gorey, a genuine eccentric who, to all who knew him, managed to have that privileged strangeness which the English have always tolerated in their wealthy classes – although he was in no large sense a public figure. Official or formal book signings, forget it. I do not believe that he ever gave public readings either or went on the circuit in order to capitalize on earnings, the way even C-list "celebrities" do nowadays. He would have agreed with poet Philip Larkin: "I don't like going about pretending to be myself."

At one point in his life, simply, Gorey had decided to go about his business and let the rest hang. He lived very like the Henry James of whom literary critic Millicent Bell once observed that "nothing, indeed, that would subsequently happen to him…no human encounter, however stirring, would alter his view of why and how he wanted to live." He was resolutely an individual, as I say, one of only two or three people I know who every minute of the day, year and year out, simply all the time, did exactly what he wanted to do.

> *Once well underground, you know exactly where you are. Nothing can happen to you, and nothing can get at you. You're entirely your own master, and you don't have to consult anybody or mind what they say. Things go on all the same overhead, and you let 'em, and don't bother about 'em. When you want to, up you go, and there the things are, waiting for you,*

said the Mole in *The Wind in the Willows*. While Gorey took refuge in no cozy realm in the deep sub-terrestrial, he was at home in a similar underground way and had the same saucerful of secrets as Moley in his hole and Ratty in the river and Badger in the wild wood and indeed dear Toad in his panting obsessions. "There is only one success – to be able to spend your life in your own way," wrote Christopher Morley in *Where the Blue Begins*, and Gorey to a large degree embodied that truth. He stood for me in that way as something of a beacon, for although he had fears, inexplicable tropisms, and surely doubts, he trusted where he wanted to go, flatly refusing to adopt conventional views, common parlance, received ideas, borrowed apocalypse. I have very little faith that any non-conformist artist – writer, painter, etc. – can succeed in the marketplace. True works of genius are always held suspect, envied, and constantly ignored. Only later do all the bootlicks assemble. It is forever the conforming, ass-kissing dufus, the obliging conventionalist, the dull predictable herbert marching in step, for whom worldly laurels are cut, shaped, awarded. Gorey received in his lifetime nothing at all like the recognition he deserved.

But he kept himself free. He joined no clubs. He adopted no one else's voice. He sang no duets. He opted for the state of being unavailable. He was not your typical, run-of-the-mill, thanks-for-taking-my-phone-call, welcome-to-my-world, have-a-nice-day chap. He lived alone all of his life. It was the way he wanted it. I always found something Kafkaesque in his suspicions of the world that kept himself well out of it. "To be chosen, to be condemned: two possible outcomes of the same process," wrote Roberto Calasso in *K.*, explaining how for hapless Joseph K. election and condemnation are almost indistinguishable. Gorey in wanting to be out of the loop needed to pursue, to find, his own resolutions. He was the freest man I know. I like to think he knew those prescient lines in Robinson Jeffers's *Dear Judas*:

> *I bid you beware of the net, fishermen.*
> *You can never see it,*
> *It flies through the white air and we are all snapped in it.*
> *No, but look round you.*
> *You see men walking and they seem to be free,*
> *But look at the faces, they're caught.*
> *There was never a man cut himself loose.*
> *… That's true but comfortless.*
> *Nor dead in their graves are not free,*
> *The mistletoe root-threads*
> *In the wood of the oak of the earth*
> *Are a net, are a net.*

I believe that Edward Gorey was a brave man, confronting what he feared in order somehow to forfend it. To me he was a worthy mentor based on that simple and convenient truth alone. I have always believed that the ultimate self-discipline comes down to this: if the bed is cold, go to bed colder. Just as all truly good writing is an assault on cliché, an individual truly to live, to be himself – "to selve," in the words of Fr. Gerard Manley Hopkins – must *avoid* stereotype at all costs, to flee the predictable, the conventional, the habitual, and to seek and find one's original self, to discover one's original meaning. Read the Gospels. It is Christ's constant plea, to be loyal to who you are and to perfect it. A self cannot be saved that is not seen. A mind is not worthy that is not studied, not searched, not seeking, not – in the Buddhist sense – "aware." What can be said to be sadder than discarded dreams? I found this in Gorey to be his essential truth, never preached to me but implicit in all he did. Once he told me he agreed with the sparkling Lorelei Lee when, in *Gentlemen Prefer Blondes*, she said, "I think that bird-life is the highest form of civilization." To me it was less a fey remark than the statement of a simple dream of peace, one he never found – or expected to find – on this earth. Flight to him was a justifiable alternative. Except for my own dear father, I honestly think I can say that I miss Edward Gorey more than anyone else I have known who has passed away.

As I say, Gorey won a Tony Award for his 1977 Broadway production of *Dracula*, starring Frank Langella, probably the only example in the history of American theater – I attended both the New York and Boston openings – in which, amazingly, the opening set was actually *applauded*! I remember well those breathtaking black-and-white sets, with a touch of red in only one place on each. Was he following the dictum of Lady Juliet Duff-Gordon who once proclaimed that every room ideally ought to contain at least one shabby object and "*une note de rouge.*" Gorey also provided illustrations for magazines as diverse as *TV Guide*, *Sports Illustrated*, *Travel and Leisure*, *The New Yorker*, and *Vogue* and of course drew the delightful opening sequences for the currently popular PBS series, *Mystery!* Eerie covers adorn many of his children's books. A Brooklyn trucking company in 1983 even requested him to draw a graveyard for their company logo. Over the years he did several covers for the *New Yorker*, some of which, he once complained to me – actually he shook his head and scornfully snorted – that they have to this day never run; I honestly cannot fathom such a blasé attitude, although that magazine is, as I understand it, frankly very much about cozy alliances as to who belongs and who does not. All politicians, as I say, bored him rigid. I also recall after that Civil War series on PBS how with true delight and twiddling

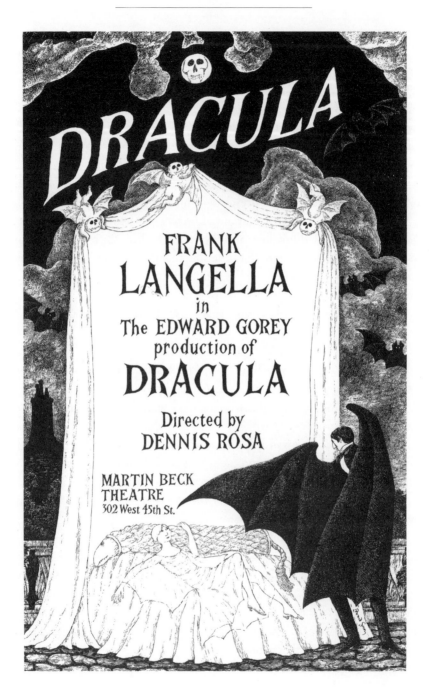

EG's *Dracula* was first performed in 1977.

fingers he mocked the "twee" hairstyle that director Ken Burns affected – he appeared to wear bangs – in all those vapid interviews he gave explaining his "genius." Curiously, Gorey never did any drawing for underground "comix," which I tend to find an odd omission in a sense, although, granted, he came from an older generation. On the other hand, in 1999 he drew the entire CD cover, front and back, for a new rock group called The Freeze, a local Cape Cod band from West Dennis, Mass., creating for them an instant collectible, of course. He also drew the cover for the Tiger Lillies, a three-piece band, formed in 1989 and based in London who were nominated for a Grammy award for their 2003 album *The Gorey End*, which was a collaboration of sorts with Gorey and the Kronos Quartet.

I find it fascinating to study in the lives of people what categories of subjects they ignore. One of those subjects with Gorey was sports. They meant absolutely nothing to him, not even to the degree that he recognized their existence as a part of human activity. I have no doubt that he knew who Babe Ruth, Jackie Robinson, and Muhammad Ali were, for they all were, among other things, national and cultural inevitabilities, but I am certain he could have told you little or nothing about them by way of fact. Football. Basketball. Golf. The America's Cup Challenge. Utter boredom for him. On the other hand, sports photographs intrigued him. "I'm always taken with sports photographs in the *New York Times*, which are not the sort of thing that anybody has really painted," he told interviewer Clifford Ross. The Olympic Games somewhat piqued his interest. This I know because we agreed that they are now completely corrupt, performed, in the face of the great 1896 charter stating that each and every participant be an amateur, by paid professional athletes, subsidized and sponsored to the hilt by international conglomerates, and all of it hard-wired into television deals with the Olympic Committee itself, which is riddled with graft. I do know that Gorey, who watched ice-skaters, characteristically rooted for hapless Tonya Harding over the huffy, self-absorbed Nancy Kerrigan during that debacle. I wonder what is being confessed in our lives, while others are madly preoccupied and watch in fascination, in what we refuse to watch as being even remotely worthwhile?

He was pronouncedly oblique in his opinions, very anti-authority, dogmatic about his tastes, a complete subversive but with a drilling conviction. He would all of a sudden pipe up with a remark, invariably serious, from the "Who'd-A-Thunk-It" school. "Airplanes have ruined opera," he once

A personal message cobbling EG's drawing of Emily Dickinson.

declared to no one in particular. "Easy flights, overbooking, lost voices. They sing themselves silly." Or "Do you seriously consider train-riding *travel?*" Portuguese poet Fernando Pessoa once said, "This may be what one calls travel, but there's nothing in it of self." "The slope is fatal, once you begin to go down it." Or "Always add a maidenhair fern with a rose." Or "Harry Langdon always made me wistful – even when he talked, as he did as mouthy Egghead in *Hallelujah, I'm A Bum!* – positively the worst movie ever made!" Or "When in Baghdad, do as the Bagdaddies do!" "Nobody ever looked better in pajamas than sweet googly-eyed Marion Davies in *The Patsy.*" Or "Andy Griffith does have a kind of inexplicable élan." Or "Surely *Salammbô* is the dullest novel ever written!" Or "Tell me, have you ever seen more perfect congruence than Bar*ba*ra Streisand's nose" – he always fully and derisively pronounced her first name with the accent on the second syllable – "and a can-opener?" And of course one of his more well-known and often repeated quotes, "When in doubt, twirl!"

I told him how I once brought a small bouquet of lilacs to a CYO class run by a strict nun, a Sister of Charity, and of my disappointment when she censoriously lifted them up with a single disapproving maneuver and blithely dropped them into a wastebasket, declaring with classic Catholic logic, "Those will put everyone to sleep!" Gorey helpfully reminded me that every time nuns appeared in movies something *bad* happened. He cited *Vertigo, Agnes of God, Heaven Knows, Mr. Allison,* as raising a minatory hand he aped a scowling nun, something along the lines of the Old Dutch Cleanser scold. "I also have a dim recollection of something frightful along those lines in *Green Dolphin Street,* where, what, Donna Reed almost gets hoovered into a rogue wave!" He burst into laughter. "What about *Come to the Stable?*" I asked, recalling one of the first movies I ever saw. "Don't the Germans shell one of their hospitals?" asked Gorey who clearly believed that nuns had lost their wimpled, billowing innocence. "One of the dear things also drives a stake though someone's waterline, doesn't she? Sister Porfirio Rubirosa, was it? The one who looked like a prison wardress on the loose!"

When tired or upset, Gorey often became ominously laconic. He tended to end conversations, as such, with a hard laugh, a sweeping gesture, a put-down, or all three at the same time. He had an arsenal of all of them. "What a loopy idea," "Not on your tintype," "It is the pits!" "I'm about to hurl!" "Are you out of your Chinese mind?" It was all of it defensive, I'm sure.

Don't come close. We don't need to share emotion. The less said the better. Haul it in. That sort of thing. His was a steady pessimism; he did not need to go through the five stages of Kübler-Ross cycle of grief. I believe his general mood was gloomy, but, from what I've seen, that's the condition, indeed the premise, of Irish humor. On the other hand, I can say that in moments of glee his face could fully brighten with the wide, upcurvital grin of Smokey Stover, his voice superadding ripples, when he'd dissolve into titivating wiggles and giggles.

I am convinced that (paradoxically) Gorey's complaints basically *disguised* his vitality, allowing him with adequate and free-ranging room to enjoy any pleasurable serendipity when and if it came, which of course it often did not. An acquaintance once admitted to me, "He does monosyllable very well." And it is true. He could be very oblique, coming at you in a slant, and even in your company remain completely inaccessible. I remember one incident for some reason, when criticizing Fred MacMurray, of Ted getting quite nettled with me. I recall the same thing happened at another time when I did a, to him, blasphemous – and no doubt bad – sinusoidally and needless to say mocking nasal impersonation of James Mason. He could also at times be very cold, matter-of-factly curt, and on many days one was not quite sure which Edward Gorey one was going to meet. There is a certain type of celebrity, often a peevish or disdainful sort in the first place, who simply looks on a true fan as an obsequious fool. Most of the time whenever I visited Gorey I felt I was disturbing him. I remember visiting him in the company of women, one a self-absorbed short person named Cathy and the other a bat-eared woman I knew named Laura, a tall, thin, sullen, unattractive hysteric with big hair, and both of them, immune to irony, raged later that he never once looked at them. He once condescendingly mocked me for being so dimly predictable as to show enthusiasm for *Cavalleria Rusticana*. "Oh, Cav/Pag," he snapped. "That!" After Edmund Wilson once castigated Gorey in print for his prose, Gorey dedicated a book to the critic that had no text. "I thought that will fix you, Edmund," Gorey harumphed. "Now what will you be able to say?" Another time Gorey chose to believe, until I quickly corrected him, that I had traduced an unmarried woman-acquaintance of his and mine, an expert in mirages, who, although I'd never kissed her or touched her or squeezed her toe, completely imagined a romantic affair with me, with Gorey later peevishly asking me, "Did you lead her down the garden path?"

He could show a touching but slightly unnerving intensity when he was exercised over something, like some nutty town-hall scheme to spray the railroad beds with poison to kill vegetation or to put up wind turbines in Nantucket Sound – the more you felt a thing, he felt, the less excuse there is for being irresponsible – when he would frustratedly keep picking up and dropping his car-keys on a table, a sound not necessarily modulated by the accompanying agitated crescendo of chatter and those big clunky rings. I do not think it is possible to account for the way he was in his separate incarnations.

"One day Anne, the boys, and I went to bleak Barnstable beach – a dark April day," my brother Paul told me. "There we saw the familiar yellow Smurf car with the joke plate, parked facing the sea. How delightful to see Gorey, I thought, whom we had hosted several times! He hid the book he was reading, but I saw that it was a new edition of some V.S. Pritchett essays. Lots of friendly greeting. Effusive on both sides. 'Let's get together!' We assumed that we would continue the talk after we looked at the beach, but no sooner had we turned our backs than he had driven away. Not mysterious. He wasn't social, felt no obligation, needed privacy and perhaps felt overwhelmed by the little family, the noise, the clamoring children. This would have been about 1982. He was like Henry James, always a guest, never a host; in demand as a guest. I remember a dinner with some friends in Dennis, around 1983. This struck me as amazingly selfish – he never brought anything and had almost no visible appreciation of whatever was served and even mocked at times, as when I served baked beans with smoked fish, English-style. One night after a chilly meal on a neighbor's porch, he came over to my house, flopped on the library sofa and exclaimed of the room, 'Its toasty warm!'"

No, Gorey would have driven away. He rarely stood around. Who was it said that the art of life is to keep down acquaintances, that one's friends one can manage, but that acquaintances could be the very devil? I always felt Gorey, hating being foisted upon, felt what Robert Frost called "freedom in departure."

Only once or twice can I say that he actually wounded me. "Sycophant," he once frostily muttered when I asked him to inscribe one of his own posters (which he did) for another illustrious cartoonist, who, let me add here, had badgered me for it: nevertheless, Gorey thought it unctuous of me, I gather, to be fertilizing one flower with another. I knew a very devoted older woman friend of his who was deeply hurt after going to the trouble to bake him a chocolate cake which she hoped to present to him as pre-arranged, with

Mr Gorey, Mr Earbrass, and a Knowledgeable Friend.

From *The Unstrung Harp.*

friends, at a local restaurant, but he had gotten wind of it and, hating to be fussed over in public, never showed up. So I have seen him enchafed, to use a word that Auden loved – irritated, not enraged. There are plenty of people in whom shyness, self-assurance, and those especially given to inexplicable fixations combine to give an uncongenial or peevish impression at times. Wittgenstein, Bertrand Russell, Philip Larkin are several distinguished examples that come to mind, characters, in the words of the wit Alan Bennett, "invariably filed under the obituarist's catch-all 'Did not suffer fools gladly.'" Gorey could indeed be petulant at times and definitely passively aggressive. If he did not want to answer the door, you could knock all day in vain, and a telephone he chose to ignore he let ring off the wall. W.H. Auden would never answer the telephone or the door bell before 1 p.m., and like Auden he liked to wear second-hand or trite (in the true Latin sense of "worn down") clothes and, well, not slippers in the street, as Wystan did, but beaten-up white sneakers. Several times I had the occasion to witness, and so in a sense feel, his arctic silences, usually at a party when someone was loud or flattering him in some ham-handed way or being annoyingly pretentious. He never became coarse or vulgar. I do not believe I ever heard him curse in a vile way, not once.

He took refuge – and even revenge – only by irony and being unavailable. I frankly never found that particularly abnormal. Didn't Nietzsche strike to the heart of a real truth when he wrote in *Beyond Good and Evil,* "Objection, evasion, distrust and irony are signs of health. Everything absolute belongs to pathology"? I do believe, however, that on the dark side Gorey sulked, was an injustice collector, and had that characteristic retributive Irish malaise when offended or slighted of staying cold and unforgiving forever in response. He controverted me. I have felt his disapproval. But I never heard the trombones take over. He never yelled. The manner of his upset was to fuss, groan, moan, sigh, tightly fold his arms against stupidity. What was sadly distressing about Gorey's arch disapproval was that, being so rare, it seemed so accurate and so true, for almost all the time he was so wistfully witty and usually so completely generous. He gave of himself all the time. It seemed he was willing to draw a poster for just about anybody, any legitimate organization – CVT-3, the Dennis Playhouse, my poetry. He allowed people to use his images. A local veterinarian has for years advertised with one of his drawings, he never sued, wouldn't think of it, just let the little mice scurry about with niblets of his cheese.

Gorey did not engage in physical exercise, none that I knew of anyway. You would not find the man bicycling or kayaking or even out taking a long walk. He didn't "do" gyms. He did not bowl. He didn't go boating, unlike the late godawful Lillian Hellman who described herself in some story as "child-happy" whenever she was sitting in a boat. He didn't play softball or baseball or watch them being played. There were several pots of leggy plants on his porch. I don't know how they got there. I never saw him garden – W. Atlee Burpee he was not – nor did I ever catch him planting tomatoes or growing dahlias or gloxinias. Mowing the lawn or grass cutting, forget it. The grass and burdock around his ocean-gray Yarmouthport house, with its single central chimney, was almost always feet long and swaying. It added to the gloom. The sunken and squeaky old front porch was wonky and broken in places, and when last I visited there a creepy poison-ivy plant – I am not making this up – was actually growing up through a slat in a back room! A raccoon family moved in to a small area in one of the back rooms, and Gorey simply let them stay. A large Southern magnolia tree can still be seen outside the kitchen as high as the house, a species, people say, growing outside its climate range. I can only add that it is part of the ongoing Gorey mystery. One summer a few years ago, in the course of writing a very long novel and having no time for exercise, I confided to Gorey that I felt fubsily overweight and wanted to take up jogging, whereupon he needled me with that gushing and sardonic laugh, exclaiming with a limp wrist, "Oh Alex, please do – before you went and puffed up last summer, you were as cute as a button!"

A passionate balletomane, Gorey was a dedicated patron of the New York City Ballet ("...anything of Balanchine... he is the City Ballet..."). He wrote and drew a quaint book called *The Lavender Leotard* (1973), the cover of which shows a ballerina whose tutu, on each and every copy, Gorey personally and painstakingly hand-painted to get the exact shade he wanted. I think I can assert without fear of contradiction that "restrained mauve" was of all the hues far and away his favorite, legendarily a gay color, true, but also a color that in its all-embracing complexity incorporates the divine and the devotional, the decadent and the *dégringolade* all at the same time. He recalled, laconically, having seen Nureyev ("a rotten dancer") in his American debut in *Don Quixote* but always had praise for the dancer Twyla Tharp, "who is," he told me in 1973, "so relentlessly avant-garde." Before he moved to Cape Cod, he was what is popularly called an "everynighter" at the City Center, watching ballets – he could always be seen at the intervals in fur coat

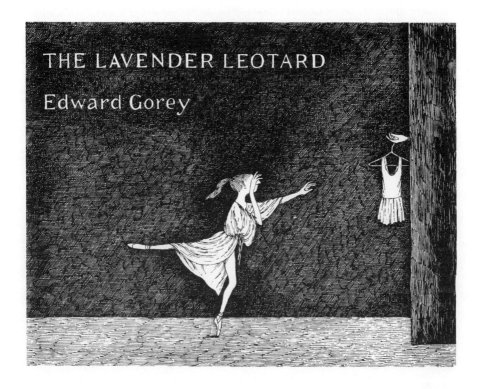

From *The Lavender Leotard.*

and Keds, according to Tobi Tobias, "in a circle of voluble friends who have exercised their territorial imperative on the bench just beyond the marble ladies of the Left Side" – and over the years he generously gave of his time to the Company, without compensation, I believe, designing many boutique items for their cause and drawing things like cups and cards, posters and potholders. He was generous to a fault. One of the reason he was often late and always behind schedule and ever forgetful was that he had said yes to too many projects and of course since he did not grind out just anything found himself overwhelmed.

"Balanchine did two or three new works a year. It's all one great glorious blur," said Gorey, "but he was the thing."

He confessed to taking, during performances of *Swan Lake*, "little naps where the corps de ballet is thrashing through it and rushing about." He told me once that he had seen a hundred and fifty *Nutcracker*s, claiming that although he loathed that Christmas ballet, he had "just got in the habit." Convince me, please. I literally tend to want to commit crimes whenever I hear snippets from that ballet, especially "The Dance of the Sugar Plum Fairies!" Duh, duh, duh, duh, da, da, da *daaa*! In the wretched excess department, I have to say I've never quite concluded whether a person who compulsively goes to so many ballets, I mean sitting there night after night, should be characterized as enthusiastic or a wheelbarrow full of crazy.

One of Gorey's most brilliant books, *The Gilded Bat* (1966), charts the brief and tragic life of a Twenties ballerina named Maudie Splaytoe, who, according to the witty legend on the dust-flap, was "discovered at the age of five by Mme. Trepidovska, forged to fineness by 100,000 pliés at the bar, polished in the provinces, acclaimed in all the capitals of Europe, established in luxury by the Baron, yet, nun-like in her devotion to The Dance, she achieves apotheosis in her immortal role, La Chauve-Souris Dorée." It is somehow always 1922 in a Gorey story. Jittery flappers with cigarette holders. Cloches. Tableaux vivants. Headbands. Pearls. Tiaras. Tennis. Berrying parties. No, he loved it. It was to ballet, if not to cats, that Edward Gorey gave, I believe, most of his adult passion. "I have to say I have always been *entiché* with gracefulness, it is so rarely found, anywhere," he once told me.

I have often considered that in a weird, extravagant way Gorey was often channeling the eccentric British writer and critic, Lytton Strachey, a tall unprepossessing bearded wit who spoke openly about his homosexuality, went as often as he could to the Russian Ballet – he personally knew, among others, Diaghilev, the Nijinskys, Lifar, and Lydia Lopokhova – was an authority on French literature but, very much like Gorey, was often too timid to speak the language, considered war to be the greatest evil, closely followed by religion, wrote at times as a theater critic, and even made efforts, poor ones, it turned out, in the direction of playwriting. He was a shy fellow and a flirt. He loved to eat and cared a good deal about the quality of food. His many letters reveal a highly complicated man, one of whose habits was to tell his mother how much he liked dressing as a woman in real life so as to confuse and entertain others. He was of course full of strong opinions and eccentric judgments, as biographies reveal – he hated telephones, the sound of his own high voice, the writing of James Joyce, Victorian prudery, and he was incipiently anti-Semitic and randomly prejudiced against blacks. Paul Levy, a Strachey Trustee and executor of his estate who edited his letters, has explained that Strachey was a cynic capable of sentimentality, a sceptic who believed in love, a charismatic wordsmith who dominated people, manipulated them to some degree, and supposedly "got his deepest joy from being the passive recipient of pain." He had an unusual relationship with the painter, Dora Carrington. Allegedly, she loved him; she committed suicide two months after his death, but Strachey was much more interested sexually in her husband Ralph Partridge, as well as in various other young men.

There was a constant tone in Gorey's voice of sweet and joyful fatigue, the upshot possibly of being incredibly busy or perhaps the result of having one of those personalities that was assailed by every quibble and quirk. "I should have finished that drawing years ago," he would say of an ignored commission, "but ennui supervened." He lapsed into chairs in a hapless, enervated way, just as though – Overcome By It All – he was ready to hand Charon his obol and pass out with a shriek of something like, "*O vanissima!*" But just as one concluded this, Gorey was suddenly alive with a vigorous observation or a laugh. "I have given up," he groaned happily, "considering happiness as relevant." His voice was lilting, coarsed high with unstrained giggles. He sputtered with ornate gestures. Frequently he wouldn't finish sentences, remaining in high and dramatic aposiopesis but like all good listeners he was full of questions for you, of the sort arranged for answers he seemed convinced would only prove once again, no matter the subject, that human behavior was getting buntier by the minute – "bunty" was another favorite word – and that we were all going to hell in a handbasket. I marveled at the way, when speaking of the decline of the

EG pointing to a just-completed, all-brown puzzle, "The Three Bears."

west, how it always seemed a given that Gorey kept himself out of the fray, an onlooker, as it were, from another planet, a man who refused to participate, to be complicit, in our folly, a satirical recorder of the world's reckless madness. He was a kind of Tiresias in that sense, a bard in the way of the *vates,* an "unacknowledged legislator of the world," as Shelley put it. I promise, I am not giving Gorey too much importance. Gorey was not a major figure in this world, but must one have to be? I wonder how many people have heard of the pre-Islamic 6th century poet Antara bin Shaddad, known as the "Black Knight" because his mother was African. The Prophet Muhammad is supposed to have commented that he had no interest in meeting any historical figure, with the *sole* exception of Antara. This amazing story cannot be found in the "Sirah" of Ibn Ishaq, which is the authoritative biography of Muhammad, but was likely one of the sayings of the Prophet. I believe that someone had put a question to Muhammad about whether he would have liked to meet anyone from the "*Jahiliyah*" ("Era of Ignorance" i.e. the time preceding Islam), and he declared, without hesitation, no one but Antara.

I have noticed all my life that those the press, the people, the *planet* ignores tend to be its most profound inhabitants, and that, sadly, those taken up, pampered, and praised are mainly hustlers, churls, opportunists. It was not that Gorey cared one way or the other. About much he showed a general sowhatsmanship and, shrugging frequently, was unconcerned about things he found do not count, like predictable attitudes and sententious people and pragmatic conversation. I would say of him what Monica Jones, a long standing lady in Philip Larkin's life, said of that strange genius of a poet: "He cared a tenth as much about what happened around him as what was happening inside him." Much of his own work Gorey even pooh-poohed, allowing himself only a real preference for two of them, his favorites, *[The Nursery Frieze]* (1964) and *[The Untitled Book]* (1971). "I do go meandering on, I have to say. When I began, I went a bit too far with my books occasionally. *The Beastly Baby* is a morbid example. I have given that up. It gets harder and harder to outrage the world. I sometimes think, what more can anybody possibly do?" Earnest people and those immune to irony wouldn't even begin to understand the man, and I can promise you fall into categories he abhorred. The maudlin, the cute, the sincere, the simple? Forget it. Indiscriminate praise embarrassed him. Gushers about his work tended to irk him. Finishing a great drawing pleased him, he told me, for about "twenty seconds." He was highly

CHAPTER ONE

Embley and Yewbert were hitting one another with croquet mallets

CHAPTER NINETEEN

They made for a huge bush

From *The Epiplectic Bicycle.*

unpredictable in his taste. Trust me, he would have much by far preferred to talk about *Petticoat Junction* episodes than your recent trip to Prince Edward Island. It was not *The Epiplectic Bicycle* he wanted to discuss, rather Anna Pavlova's *pizzicati* on tiptoe and the power of her lovely ankle and toes of steel that made her steadily held, exquisite pauses possible.

"I've never been *anywhere*," Gorey confessed. That was a fact. But this will positively astound the Gorey devotee: he never once traveled to England, the zany locale of his almost every book, etched, as each is, in as graphically and scrupulously British a manner as could be found in the drawings of Cruikshank or Phiz. Gorey's is an almost exclusively late-Victorian, Edwardian, or 1920s domain, a closed world set in out-of-the-way places like Collapsed Pudding; Miss Underfoot's Seminary; Willowdale; Penwiper Mews; the Crampton Vinegar Works; Dogtown; Hiccupboro; Penetralia; and so forth – and the dedicated reader, if at first amazed, soon finds all nicely appointed: mustachioed gents in greatcoats and ankle-length mufflers, barons, mad for new diversions; shunting yards; truculent aunts; etiolated families in crumbling English mansions; deranged nannies brandishing pokers; croquet fields; gasometers; lonely and desolate handcars; secretive dark-eyed vamps with furbelows and long cigarette holders; boaters; old chappies in plus-fours; pie-faced ingenues, with pyknic builds dying for art. Every woman seems to be a version of a Twenties flapper, long-limbed, kohl-eyed Nancy Cunard-types, wearing a bell-like cloche and ropes of pearls, always jitteringly smoking a cigarette in a long holder, while his male characters are either mustachioed and well-muscled stalwarts wearing heavy cardigans or self-conscious bumblers in long scarves or scary, overbearing creatures with black homburgs and eerie interests. There is a distinct genre here.

A foul murder has usually been committed. Or someone has disappeared. A prelate with a cruel smirk exposes himself to a toddler. A face is missing from the stained-glass window or church. A message is left in a pile of brussels sprouts. Searches go on endlessly. Sinister plots are often carried along by strange objects – urns, bell-pulls, white cards, peculiar messages – and scattered clues. There are black dolls, hideous insects, misplaced gloves, lost objects, slips of paper, flashlights, and no end of inexplicable creatures. Hatpins figure in his plots. So do arsenical buns and grisly secateurs. And wallpaper. (*The West Wing*, for all practical purposes, could serve as a legitimate wallpaper "sample" book for prospective decorators.) Décor is description in Gorey. One finds the ghostly recurrent image of someone on a tall bicycle pedaling through the autumn mist. I am convinced that a Ph.D. dissertation will one day be written entitled, "The Significance of the Bicycle in Edward Gorey's Work," a particular conveyance that figures as much in his work as it does in Samuel Beckett's. But then the same might be said of veils and doors and empty rooms. Or topiary. Or bloaters. Or statuary. Or symbolic stones. An herb is discovered in one story that grows only in rock crevices on Mt. Dormitor. Personages in these tales have heads like prunes or are faceless, a solitary man clad only in pajama bottoms is lost on a moor, baleful child-molesters aggregate to fumble each other in cold woodsheds, and flappers, looking tenuous, as pages turn rarely seem to belong to various mise-en-scènes.

"I am known for fogs and murderous vapors in my books," he once said to me, adding, "Don't ask me why." Was it not that atmosphere figured so largely in his books? "Do they mean the trace gases that suffuse the faces of all those people in such a ghastly way in *The Day the World Ended* starring handsome blond Richard Denning who was in every science-fiction movie that ever was, do you think?"

There is in Gorey's work an ambience, English to be sure, of whispers, murders, and unnatural acts – where orphans are hobbled, *objets* disappear, and things go phut quietly (but always in a ghastly way) in overripe and diseased gardens, at rail sidings, or – yes – in the pea soup of thick London Particulars, where droolies and drazels, lizardlike, crooked, and adroit, go creeping down the alleys. Gorey, in an isolation reminiscent of Kant's, saw into the life of the world beyond him, solely through his voracious reading. As I said, almost every one of the rooms in his house, except the back kitchen, was piled high with books, *crammed* with them, high swaying columns, ziggurats – there was something like 30,000 of them at the end. (After his death, the library was sold in 2009 to the University of California at San Diego.) Knowledge, he treasured. Most people do not read. There were special piles of books to be read, I mean books he bought and was nervously driven to get to, and, as I say, he read *everything*, outré things like the works of Oliver Onions, the poet Jones Very, Mrs. Oliphant – remote English novels from the 1880s like *Adam Graeme* or *He That Will Not When He May* – and people like Capt. Marryat, George Farquhar, E. C. Benson. "*What can be delaying that young madcap?*" Gorey once cheerfully proclaimed when I showed up late for a visit. I looked puzzled at the reference; he waved, "Oh that's a line from Edith Bishop Sherman's *Mistress Madcap Surrenders*" and went padding back into the back room, as I followed. *That* was his world. I mention here, however, that I do not think Edward Gorey knew his Bible very well.

His grasp of British idiom was quite astonishing. I first laid eyes on a Gorey book in London in 1968, in a small Knightbridge bookshop to be specific, and bought it, believing that the brilliant author whose work referred itself to the last century was obviously a contemporary of other great British artists and illustrators such as Hilaire Belloc and Edward Lear and George Cruikshank. His characters taken all together make up a neo-Dickensian onamasticon, with a cast of wonderlings such as Mr. Earbrass; Udgeion; Miss Squill; Professor Bedsock; Ursula Schnittlauch; Snibby; Maudie Splaytoe, Miss Underfold, Luke Touchpaper; the wheelchair killer, Nurse J. Rosebeetle; lumberjack Sarah Jane ('Batears') Olafsen; Mrs. Fledaway; Harold Snedleigh; Mona Gritch; the Baron de Zabrus; the MacFizzets; Plastikoff; Mona Skrim-Pshaw; Mr.Crague; Millicent Frastley; Miss Marshgrass; Eepie Carpetrod; Rose Marshmary, Mary Rosemarsh, and Marsh Maryrose, Figbash; and of course the lovely ballerina, Federojenska. Nobody – no one – loved names more than Edward Gorey.

"I got interested in puppeteering by reading Seneca's plays," he told me. "I thought wouldn't it be fun to do Seneca with puppets." He made his puppets out of Celluclay, always baking and painting them himself, tight little white squirrel-sized heads with winsome faces that looked like his drawings.

Several characters that have appeared in some of the puppet-plays held in various tiny theaters around Cape Cod over the last decade have names like Aubergine; Arthur Hooka; Hooded Personage; Hissie, the Clueless Widow and utter mad things like "O God! O Montreal!" and "I'm all for people being veiled," and "The memory of my ashes will consolation be: Then farewell, Tuscarora, and farewell, sir, to thee." By the way, Gorey had to act on stage one summer in one of his highly stylized plays – thank God, not in his wild neo-Byzantine stage-play, *Oscar Wilde's Salome,* which was done completely in drag – when one of his local actors became ill, but Ted, being somewhat nervous, was so bird-voiced, so diffident, so mutteringly hard to hear, that he won no hearts. Henry Irving he was not. Maybe Colley Cibber. I have never seen anyone work so hard as Gorey-as-dramaturge did, however. Six weeks of rehearsal in any given play were usually followed by three weeks of production. The dear man not only wrote, directed, and designed the plays, but he actually made all of the puppets, and then of course drew the posters, from which handbills were usually made – there was a time when he even helped distribute them! – driving long distances every night to each performance. I don't remember him ever missing a single night during these endless productions. It might be mentioned here that in 1996 Gorey designed an amazing set for a performance of *Hamlet* on Cape Cod at the old Cotuit Center for the Arts (since burned down), a strictly 501-c3 (non-profit) staging that starred as the Prince a brilliant Gorey actor named Vincent Mayotte. The set was all black, white, and gray. I remember how the cast, many of them, used to visit the local Kettle-Ho bar to swap notes and drink beers, and I even watched one rehearsal when, after one of the actors became ill, Gorey, filling in, not spectacularly but wittily read for Ophelia, and, muffling a laugh now as I did then, I can still hear him – with sibilants stressed – utter, "Where is the beauteous Majesty of Denmark?" and "My lord, as I was sewing in my closet, Lord Hamlet, with his doublet all unbrac'd..." and "There's fennel for you, and columbines. There's rue for you, and here's some for me. We may call it herb of grace o' Sundays...."

Gorey was probably emotionally unhealthy, like one of those characters in the stories of Joris Karl Huysmans or Heinrich Kleist or Villiers de L'Isle-Adam, if the key to emotional health is "connectedness," to use the kind of contemporary buzzword that always seems to sanction the crass communal behavior of every glad-handing loudmouthed Rotarian or crazed, ginned-up Amway salesman pumping your hand or any half-assed political drummer. Our friend was different. The father of Prince André in *War and Peace*, old Prince Bolkonsky, with his dogged and curmudgeonly pursuits insistently comes to mind. I believe that if the key to emotional health means blithely giving yourself away to neighbors or opening your door to any dipshit in a hat who wants to stop in for coffee – as if solitude cannot supply the fullness of unity! – then Edward Gorey was in less trouble than most, but in the last decade of his life he did bond with many of the actors in his plays, and several were quite close to him. I remember he would drive twenty miles to Wood's Hole, direct rehearsals to a play, then drive twenty miles back, every night. I found many of the puppet-plays sort of silly, overdone. He made the papier-maché puppets, wrote the scripts, devised the sets, and designed the now highly collectible posters he signed and sold, always handing over the proceeds to the theater. I don't think he cared a jot about money. He never had much. It meant virtually nothing to him.

His plays, *Lost Shoelaces, Tinned Lettuce, A Blithering Christmas, Inverted Commas, Crazed Teacups, Flapping Ankles, The Ides of Mohonk, A Wake,*

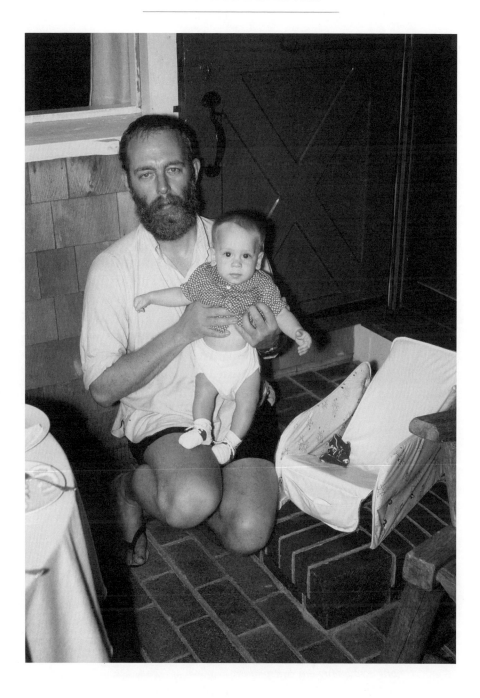

EG holding baby Kenny Morton, ca. 1968.

Wallpaper, Helpless Doorknobs, Chinese Gossip, Heads Will Roll, English Soup, etc. – the names, evoking the ephemeral, might have been his hedge against their public failures – were always performed for very small but appreciative audiences, often made up friends and acquaintances, at $3.00 or so a ticket, usually in stifling little *boîtes,* outlying theaters, or small rooms where the audiences were fairly sparse for the most part. There was a lot of Kukla-Fran-and-Ollie about them, human interchange with puppets. Some were musicals, several were costume dramas, and one was even done in drag! When one of the actors was indisposed because of illness or whatever, Gorey would happily stand in for him or even her. (A great actor he was not.) I remember seeing middling performances in places like the Magical Oyster Theater in Wood's Hole, at the Theater-by-the-Bay in Bourne, several at the Provincetown repertory Theater, one even in a small side-room in a hotel on Route 28 in Hyannis. Several of his plays were originally performed in New York and even in London. I have tried to trace down a play he supposedly wrote at Harvard in 1952 called *Amabel; or, The Partition of Poland,* but I have had no luck.

In the fall of 2000, *The White Canoe,* Gorey's "opera seria for hand puppets," was posthumously performed at Freedom Hall in Cotuit. After he died a libretto was found in his house based on a ghoulish ballad by Thomas Moore called "The Lake of the Dismal Swamp." Music was written for it by Daniel J. Wolf and five months after his death another play of Gorey's was on stage and ran for a month, with Joan Kirchner, soprano, and Thom Dutton, tenor Herbert Senn and Helen Pond designed a magnificent set. Let the following snippets from Moore's poem give some indication of how suitably the tale fit the Gorey canon.

> *They made her a grave, too cold and damp*
> *For a soul so warm and true;*
> *And she's gone to the Lake of the Dismal Swamp,*
> *Where, all night long, by a fire-fly lamp,*
> *She paddles her white canoe.*
>
> *And her fire-fly lamp I soon shall see,*
> *And her paddle I soon shall hear;*
> *Long and loving our life shall be,*
> *And I'll hide the maid in a cypress tree,*
> *When the footstep of death is near.*

Cotuit Center for the Arts

presents

THE WHITE CANOE

AN OPERA SERIA FOR HAND PUPPETS

libretto by Edward Gorey
music by Daniel J. Wolf

director C. J. Verburg   music director Thom Dutton

FREEDOM HALL, 975 MAIN STREET, COTUIT

8 PM Fridays and Saturdays, 7 PM Sundays
September 1 - 23, 2000
no performance Saturday, September 9

Adults $12   Children $6
Member discount $2

RESERVATIONS 428-0669

EG's *White Canoe* was first performed in 2000.

One would have thought that, over the years, Gorey waking up in a vast bedroom with an heraldic shield or two, after a breakfast of buttered kippers, rashers of bacon, kidneys, haddock kedgeree, liver steaks, poached eggs, and slices of toast – a sort of *déjeuner dînatoire,* as the French used to call it long ago – had systematically snapped on his windcheater, trundled himself out in cold rains, and, notebook in hand, effortlessly pilgrimaged the English world from its stews to its coombs and moors to its closed-circuit baronial estates. But Gorey's was the England of the Anglophile: of myth, of fantasy, of caricature. I know that he loved Evelyn Waugh's novel *Brideshead Revisited,* published in 1945, and that it has been said that the book had a major influence on him. Nothing in Gorey's work fully encompassed his sanctuary Yarmouthport, his adopted New York, or the plains or cities of his native Midwest. He did once tell me, however, "Willa Cather can still make me weepy."

I know several people regard the "England" of his books as mere pastiche, third-hand Anglomania, all the talk about "the village" and having tea or Bovril or Epp's cocoa and all the weird urns, hedges, and topiary. Many who dismiss it all as borrowed apocalypse rendered from books, and not good books, despite the fact that it is diabolically clever, also argue quite vehemently that he cannot possibly have spent more than five minutes in the shires that he writes about and illustrates. In a sense, however, the comedy arises specifically from its being derivative, giving it a tighter stringency. Gorey has not a large audience in England that I know of, not a major one, in any case, in the same way that the Tarzan books are not read in Africa. He is a bit like one of his gurus, Arthur Waley, orientalist, translator of Tang poetry, who deliberately did not go to China, because he did not want his illusions shattered.

As I say, traveling – anywhere – did not really interest Gorey. On the other hand, I suppose it may be argued that compulsive readers do little else, at least in their dreams. "I wouldn't mind seeing China if I could come back the same day," the poet Philip Larkin once drolly quipped, a remark that Gorey might have made. That China idea fits. I believe that, as to travel, he followed Gertrude Stein's stay-at-home logic – "In China there is no need of China, because in China china is china." No, travel was not his bliss. Gerhard Mercator may indeed have "flattened" the globe, fine – it would still not have tempted Edward Gorey to get up and go. He liked New England weather. He did not want to live in the square states or experience the Deep South or drive around in the bitter brown sunlight of California. "Nothing, like something, happens anywhere." Larkin also once superbly remarked, and in a very real sense he was quite correct. Immanuel Kant never traveled more than a hundred miles from Königsberg. Henry David Thoreau who was relatively provincial in his travels through the country – "I have a real genius for staying at home" – never crossed the ocean. Goethe never rode on a railway train, never sailed on a steamship, never saw Paris, never saw London, never saw St. Petersburg, never saw Vienna, and caught but a fleeting glimpse of Berlin but, according to Georg Brandes "was within himself a whole and complete civilization." We all remember Thoreau's wonderful paradox: "I have traveled much in Concord." On the other hand, touching on the subject of travel, Gorey did once admit to me that there were indeed three specific places that could have lured him abroad to see: (1) the Ryōan–ji Zen temple and gardens in northwest Kyoto, Japan; (2) the monstrous Bomarzo Stones, near Orte in the province of Viterbo in Italy – a huge screaming moon-face is perhaps its best-known icon – where weird mossy monoliths of tortoises and grimacing creatures, all hewn God knows when, timelessly squat: and (3) the ante-room, designed by Michelangelo, of the Biblioteca Laureziana in Florence, where the columns are recessed and there is strangely no interplay at all between surface and architectural elements. These are the only places that Edward Gorey wished to visit, no others, and there was an end to it. As to books?

What did he not read? He read virtually everything. It was by reading alone that he traveled and kept him abreast of the waking world. I remember one time taking a walk with him down in my town of West Barnstable on Sandy Neck Beach (a peninsula in New England is called a "neck") – "In your weekly *déménagement* from here to teach at Harvard," he once asked me, pointing, "are you not tempted to set up a small fo'castle out on these dunes to see out your days?" – to which we had repaired to walk off the sleepy effects of a large meal I had cooked. I occasionally look to find stones along the beach to try to discern the odd face in them, animal or human, a habit I had picked up from the late great wood-engraver Fritz Eichenberg. When a small wave trickled in on my shoes, I quoted,

Oh, how I wanted to compete
with the tumultuous breakers dying
in adoration at her feet!
Together with those waves – how much
I wished to kiss what they could touch!

Alicia and the Sea Monster

Greed, Complacency, and the
Busy Repairman frolic against
the sun setting, probably
forever, over Cape Cod

Top photo: A seashell drawing.

Bottom photo: Illustration for an article on Cape Cod by Alexander Theroux.

"Pushkin," said Gorey. "Translated by?" "Let me guess – Mr. Nabokov." I was amazed. "Was it the foot imagery, your deep knowledge of Russian literature, *Eugene Onegin* in particular, that novel in verse, or a combination of all?"

He paused.

"Let's go with feet."

The writing of Ronald Firbank, the English novelist, he of the precious, witty, and campily gnomic eight or so novels, Gorey cited as "the greatest influence on me." "Oh," he laughed, "because he is so concise and so madly oblique." Again, because of the passionate and enthusiastic exaggerations he brought to almost every opinion, one could never be sure Gorey was not simply exercising a mirthful option. But prodded to it, he listed among his favorite authors – fraticellians, clearly – Anthony Trollope; Theodore Dreiser; Lady Murasaki; Willa Cather; the "Lucia" books of the prolific Edwardian, E. F. Benson; Samuel Beckett and Jorge Luis Borges; and especially Jane Austen. "Jane Austen knew more about everything than anybody else who ever lived – just how awful it really is underneath," he told *Newsweek* in 1977. He believed in the dark at the top of the stairs. "I never could understand why people always feel they love to climb up Mount Everest when you know it's quite dangerous getting out of bed." I remember him once exclaiming for weeks over Marjorie Kennan Rawlings's *The Yearling,* and finding creepiness in it. Francis Ponge, Max Jacob, and Raymond Queneau are three French writers he was especially taken with. "I find E.D.E.N. Southworth charming. Sara Orne Jewett. And Mrs. Molesworth, of course." He hummed as he pondered. High-culture Gorey and low-culture Gorey were a single movement, criss-crossing in a single conversation like bat flight. "I adore the English girl's school stories of Angela Brazil. When I find a new Nancy Drew, of course, you can't tear me away from it. I detest Henry James – one of the worst writers. Oh, abominable, don't you agree? He went downhill when he started all that dictation." Gorey splayed out in his chair, moaned, and looked up. "I've read virtually everything he's written."

I have often thought that Gorey himself actually resembled to a degree Jane Austen, who was something of a recluse and content with her spinster's domestic life. An artist of irony and exceptional wit, she traveled very little, and never very far at that, but read widely and with passion – she knew Fielding, Smollett, Sterne, and Richardson thoroughly – but for her own curiosity, gossip, and literary ends opted to learn about London, Bath,

Salisbury, Southampton, and other fashionable places from the second-hand accounts of a country cousin. Another dissertation here, no?

I was lucky enough in 1973 to see Edward Gorey's old workroom at his cousin's house on Millway in Barnstable when he lived there. It was an attic, actually, very like a lair, at the very top of the house overlooking the blue harbor, a small wooden Raskolnikovian affair with three windows letting in sunlight (or moonlight). There he drew all of his books prior to 1988 – cratchited to a low stool, penciling out his delicately detailed characters and finicky configurations, crosshatched and elegant. He carefully inked everything with special imported pen-points from England called Gillott Tit Quills, the supply of which he was afraid, for some reason, would run out. I remember noticing three or four unfinished pencil sketches on his desk: the fat, un-get-at-able impish faces of his characters with their pin-point eyes or questioning black-circled orbs and disturbing semi-malevolent half-smiles, seemed to peer out uncannily like tiny tragic planets. Consider the textures in a Gorey drawing, how he could do anything with line and space, often daring plaid jackets against a wallpaper patterned of roses or triangles. Open *The West Wing* (1963) or *The Blue Aspic* (1968) or *The Prune People* (1983) or *L'Heure Bleue* (1975) to see some of the most astonishing combinations of patterns in the history of interior decoration! Edward Gorey's wallpaper patterns should be patented. He adored wallpaper. "*The Umbrellas of Cherbourg* was full of baroque wallpaper," he once told me, referring to one of his favorite films in regard to something I had said of plaid. We had been discussing color, I recall, and I made reference to the hue of a Tunisian city when he quickly observed with almost Proustian neurasthenia, "I get physically sick from too much red." Study the skies in his books, the amazing range of moods he invested in them. They are overcast Rorschachs, never one the same. He could draw water with uncanny insight. And space? He used it with as much skill, in counterpoint and in contrast, as did Picasso, an artist, by the way, with whom Gorey, characteristically referring to him as "the greatest cultural villain of all," had small patience and less love. "I think he is sentimental and not much else," pronounced Gorey. "And that would include *Guernica*, folks, a painting I couldn't wait for them to send back somewhere else. I'm just out of sympathy with it." I remember asking him in 1998, twitting him a bit, if he planned to attend the Early Picasso exhibition that had just gone up at the Museum of Fine Arts in Boston. Groaning, Gorey flapped a hand and muttered, "I'd rather die." Andrew Wyeth is another great painter Gorey had small sympathy with, a convention with many modern artists, one I fail to understand.

The formal procedure he employed in creating a book was always to do the text first. "If I start doing the drawings before the text is finished, something happens to the book and it disappears," he said. So he always tried to have the writing well under way, if not finished, before he started to draw. One need only look at the unique layouts, all the detailed cross-hatching, and the amazingly complicated pen-and-ink work to see how long one of his more Byzantine drawings could take, sometimes three a day. To look at the fine line work in Gorey's brilliant drawings is to understand why Charles Dickens, in an after-dinner speech, once defined genius as "an infinite capacity for taking pains." I can say that Gorey more than kindly drew two original book-jackets for me, astonishing work, and to see an original Gorey up-close is an event. He was the master of ink drawing. He worked on drawings with India ink on Strathmore paper in the exact size they appear in all of his books, usually four inches by five inches. He told me that he once tried drawing on a computer but said derisively that most of his efforts came out like Matisse. I looked to see if he was smiling. Nope.

"My favorite painter, when push comes to shove, is Goya. And I guess I'd pick [watercolorist Charles] Burchfield as my favorite American artist. Pulsating nature. Such ghostliness. He listened to Sibelius and pondered the existence of God. I also love Albert York, whom nobody has heard of, hardly. He does some landscapes. He does cows. He's very good at cows. He does 'still lives' in sort of tin cans."

Gorey, who generally tended to dislike much that was contemporary – most newcomers to his work tend to think that he is a long-dead Victorian illustrator – once mentioned to me that among his favorite contemporary painters, both intentionally marginal men as well as elegant allegorists of angst, were Balthus and Francis Bacon, painters whose canvased vision of heaven is, arguably, essentialized by looking down on the damned in hell. I have often wondered what Gorey so loved in Balthus, other than the fact that they both adored cats and worshipped Mozart. The muffled violence? The sexual tension? The anti-bourgeoisification of his view? The ambiguity? The discomforting facts of children's sexuality? The zombie-like self-absorption in the faces of compromised young girls? (Is it not ironic that Gorey, who knew nothing of children, was, like Henry James, so preoccupied with their tiny lives?) Gorey expressed admiration for Gustave Doré, Sir John Tenniel, Ernest Shepard, and A. A. Milne, adding that he felt a great affection for the many "highly visual" wood engravings found in nineteenth-century Gothic and Romantic novels as well as the "problem" pictures and anecdotal illustrations which the Victorians so cherished. He admired Victorian sand paintings and kept several examples in his living room, postcard-sized pictures of English views mounted in glazed oak frames. And remember Albert York, whose cows Gorey has previously rhapsodized about, a reclusive painter of small, mysterious landscapes who not only shunned the art world but usually wrapped his paintings in brown paper and mailed them to the gallery. Any contemporary illustrators that he admired? "Yes," offers Gorey, "I very much like two Englishmen, Edward Bawden and Edward Ardizzone."

A kind of "model man" repeats in his work – a muscular, aged, ballet-dancer type, bearded, odd footwear, maybe a girl's ideal man (father type). A question is, were these him or was he looking up to them? Who was the master and who the slave? His mode of being was girlish in essence. "Silly me, I can say anything" was the message. Little girls (often tragic) figure in his work; he strongly identified with them in some strange way and sometimes punished them. There was always an inner narrative – behavioral, filial, psychological – going on below or beside or above any given text of Gorey's that the average reader had not a clue about. I have always thought the tall, stalwart, bearded men in Gorey's drawings – you will often find them sporting great black hearty mustaches and collegially wearing long heavy woolen turtleneck sweaters that fall well past the hips – had the same strange Mannerist elongations that Michelangelo's figures do, a like musculature, at times even the women, and the character Chubb's witty iterations in Alan Bennett's hilarious play, *A Question of Attribution,* could have been addressing the same odd physiologies of Gorey's characters when he says, "Titian's beard is so badly done it looks as if it hooks on behind the ears" and "I don't think they are all that lifelike, frankly. The women aren't. They're just like men with tits, and the tots look as if they've been put on with an ice-cream scoop. Has nobody pointed that out?"

He personally owned a couple of Vuillard drawings, a Bonnard drawing, one Munch lithograph, a Berthe Morisot etching of a lady with a cat, as well as a Klee etching, and ten Atget photographs in tarnished brass frames. I know that he also liked the work of Max Ernst and his original *"grattage"*

There's a rather odd couple in Herts
Who are cousins (or so each asserts);
    Their sex is in doubt
    For they're never without
Their moustaches and long, trailing skirts.

From *The Listing Attic*.

EG and furry friend in his attic, 1961.

technique. I once took a wood-block in a fit of architectural art a decade or so ago and made a jail out of it – carved it, painted it black, fashioned barred windows, and so forth – and it was no small source of flattery to me that when Gorey asked me if I would make him one, I did so, and it sat on one of the shelves in his house to the end. I never saw a painting in Gorey's house, notable or not, small or large, watercolor or oil, that was not superb. He had an exquisite sense of selection. He once told me regretfully that he once had a chance to purchase an actual Francis Bacon at a good price but failed to.

Although he admitted to having had one particularly influential art teacher in high school, for the record Gorey said, "My great-grandmother – my mother's father's mother – is the single person, I guess, from whom I inherited my talent. Or" – he shrugged, exhaling that despairing sigh – "whatever you want to call it." I was curious. "Helen St. John Garvey was her name," he explained. "She supported the family in the middle of the last century by, oh, illustrating greeting cards and writing mottoes." Apparently she was at one time very well known for the Christmas cards she painted for the old McClurg's in Chicago. At the time her old diploma, looking like a medieval spice chart, hung directly over Gorey's work desk in that old Barnstable house, and some of her watercolors also hung on the walls there. I still remember the late afternoon of that first interview. Agrippina, having sniffed us out, leapt familiarly to his lap. Gorey stroked her tenderly to sleep, a slant of coppery sun, coming through the window from Barnstable Harbor, shining through the little flanges of the cat's ears. I could have painted the scene.

Directly across from this room was *that* room: an old curiosity shop of a chamber, crepuscular as hell. It looked like an old rookery. As I say, Gorey was quite a magpie and loved old landscapes, unique signs, orts and sorts of all kinds. This was your legendary Goreyesque room: a jumble of antiques, humped chests, sea stones, hempen figures, candlesticks, pots and potsticks, glass eggs, skulls and skeletons of all shapes and sizes (sent to him by admirers? alchemized? snatched out of crypts?), and, of course, row upon row of frogs, wooden, ceramic, and beanbag. It was all of it a gorgeous clutter, and one could almost feel within the place the ghostly presence of some of his own creatures, like the Throbble Spectre, the Wuggly Ump, Beelphazor, the Raitch, and the Doubtful Guest, that enduring penguin-like oddity in white tennis-shoes who never goes away. There is also the Quingawaga that squeaks and moans while dining off of ankle bones. And how about the Zote? "About the Zote what can be said? There was just one, and now it's dead."

This, of all the mysterious sites, would most thoroughly enchant members of the Gorey cult – it is nothing less – now numbering, I would guess, in the tens of thousands, diligent collectors of both his limited editions, and more easily available books. The Gorey House peddles all sorts of Goreyana, which one can also find on-line, including Gorey cups, Gorey posters, Gorey writing paper, Gorey buttons, Gorey notepads, Gorey postcards, Gorey wallpaper, Gorey rubber hand-stamps, Gorey calendars, Gorey stickers, Gorey date-books, Gorey bookmarks, Gorey bean bags, Gorey shoelaces, and Gorey Christmas cards. There are also available Gorey mousepads, jewelry, totebags, laser cels, magnets, neckties, puzzles, Tarot cards, and mini-lunchboxes. A set of sterling silver Gorey bat cuff-links is presently selling for $80. A series of nine "Elephantômas" etchings, available online, is being hawked for as much as $17,500. I recall reading how Thomas Merton (Fr. Louis) was mortified, even indignant, that the Trappist monks got into the commercial business of selling everything from jellies to cheese, fruitcakes to honey, bread to CDs of their Gregorian chants. I believe Gorey would have felt the same with all these marketing ploys and wholesale exploitation of his work. New York's Gotham Book Mart & Gallery, with whom he first published *The Sopping Thursday* (1970), handled Goreyana (books printed, many of them, by the Fantod Press, Gorey's own imprint, cost a fortune now) but also the sixty or so other books that he brilliantly illustrated, including works of Charles Dickens, Edward Lear, Lewis Carroll, Raymond Chandler, Samuel Beckett, John Ciardi, and T. S. Eliot. A printed bibliography of all of Edward Gorey's work, which was constantly updated, had been available through the Book Mart and included a listing of pretty much everything he did, *including* various foreign translations such as Swiss, German, Swedish, Italian, and Dutch.

Very few artists come to mind who have combined, whether successfully or not, both writing and drawing. (Many believe he was as good a writer as an artist.) Gorey's mastery of this idiom is perhaps best located in his longest work, *The Unstrung Harp* (1953), a "novel" of thirty pages dealing with the problem of writing a novel, all in the portrait-of-the-artist mode; it is almost word-perfect, to my mind, and will remain certainly one of the finest miniature prose works ever. Mr. Clavius Fredrick Earbrass, our hero and far and away one of Gorey's most memorable characters, "belongs," in the author's words, to the straying, rather than to the sedentary, type of author. He is never to be found at his desk unless actually writing down a sentence. Before this happened he broods over it indefinitely while picking up and putting down again small, loose objects: walking diagonally across rooms; staring out of windows; and so forth. He frequently hums, more in his mind than anywhere else, themes from the Poddington Te Deum.

As I say, I never believed that in his lifetime Edward Gorey got anything like the attention he deserved. To mention the critical neglect of Gorey is not a commonplace. Edmund Wilson, in the *New Yorker*, was the first to recognize Gorey's genius, although Wilson criticized, nigglingly, the French in some of Gorey's limericks; that was then followed, hardly soon, by a random burst of often misinformed and tiny profiles and feuilletonistic bits and pieces in the late Sixties and early Seventies, each one curiously asseverating that a new talent was being discovered; that the macabre albums and deathful pamphlets now so recognizably Gorey's and Gorey's alone were marvelous; but that, shoot, they couldn't be slotted anywhere. What was the genre? Fiction? Fable? This book is wordless! That one is one-inch high! That one pops up! This one folds the wrong way! *The Pointless Book*; or *Nature & Art* (1993), a matchbox-sized book – and thumbable! – is 64 pages of framed indecipherable squiggles. And, look at this muddled series of postcards – and all unsequenced at that! How should they be filed in libraries – under *art*? And in bookstores was "humor" the right department? They weren't children's books, were they? But they seem to be, don't they? And so on and so forth. Gorey always simply shrugged and kept on working, which is exactly what artists do.

The cult, he always said, affected him "adversely," in that he felt, among other things, "terribly guilty about not answering letters." And, who knows, possibly he was sent skulls through the post. Or invited to black masses, or perhaps he found his books being sent back in the mail shredded by indignant mothers.

"Terribly guilty," repeated Gorey, hugging his knees and looking wispish and forlorn.

In 1973 I remember finishing my interview with him. It was getting dark. The glimpse of sky, paid out through Gorey's attic window, showed itself a murk of darkening gray-blue wash. Shadows within elongated. I was ready to be off. Gorey stood up across from me, and the soft dusk showed him, now, even more of a twilight figure, for the eyes in his semi-gaunt face were also shadowed over, next to invisible, and – very like the eyes found cross-hatched and smudged in his long-suffering little characters – appeared in the dim light only as deep, deep hollow sockets: two dark windows, shades drawn.

A last question that should have been my first: I asked him, awkwardly, as I recall, as I stood in the doorway, why he thought that stark violence and horror and terror were the uncompromising focus of his work.

"I write about everyday life," came Gorey's simple reply, out of a shadow.

On Wednesday, April 13, 2000 – and he made no bones about feeling both ill at ease and alienated from the whole idea of the new millennium – Edward Gorey had a massive heart attack. A neighbor and friend from Cummaquid, Rick Jones, who had just fixed an electrical appliance for him, turned and said regarding his fee, "Well, Ted, that'll be twenty dollars you owe me." Gorey, who had been sitting on his sofa, immediately flung his head back which made Jones think in light of his remark that Gorey was joking. He had had trouble with his heart before, small irregularities, and doctors on Cape Cod at one time had considered giving him a pacemaker, but nothing was done that way. After Jones called 911, the EMTs came immediately and took Gorey to the Hyannis hospital, where he died at 6:30 p.m. on Saturday, April 15th at the age of 75. His body was cremated, and his ashes were strewn over the waters at Barnstable Harbor on a day overcast and gray and hammering with rain.

Alexander Theroux has taught at Harvard, MIT, Yale, and the University of Virginia, where he took his doctorate in 1968. A Fulbright, Guggenheim, and National Endowment of the Arts fellow, he is the author of four highly regarded novels – *Three Wogs* (1972), *Darconville's Cat* (1982), *An Adultery* (1987), and *Laura Warholic, or The Sexual Intellectual* (2009) – and of several books of essays, fables, travel, and poetry. He lives in West Barnstable, Massachusetts with his wife, the artist Sarah Son. He has twice been nominated for the National Book Award.